Raw Painting

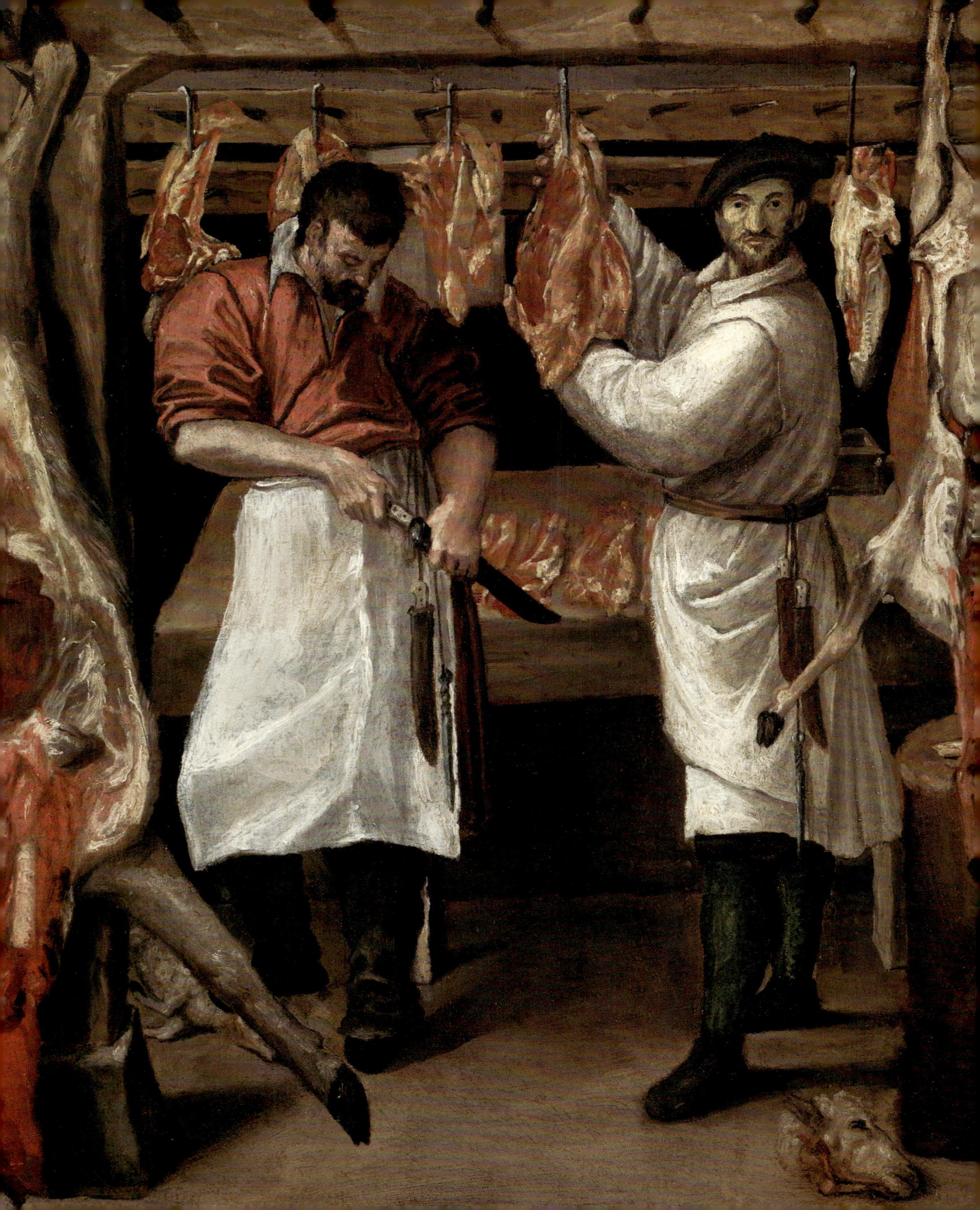

KIMBELL MASTERPIECE SERIES

Raw Painting

The Butcher's Shop
by Annibale Carracci

C. D. DICKERSON III

Kimbell Art Museum
Fort Worth

DISTRIBUTED BY
Yale University Press
New Haven and London

Published by the Kimbell Art Museum, Fort Worth
Distributed by Yale University Press, New Haven and London

Kimbell Art Museum
3333 Camp Bowie Boulevard
Fort Worth, Texas 76107-2792
www.kimbellart.org

Yale University Press
302 Temple Street
P.O. Box 209040
New Haven, Connecticut 06520-9040
www.yalebooks.com

Produced by the Publications Department of the Kimbell Art Museum
Wendy P. Gottlieb, Manager of Publications
Megan Smyth, Publications and Editorial Assistant
With thanks to Robert LaPrelle, Judy Mahan, Mark Marr, and Karen Powelson

Designed by Tom Dawson

Printed in Singapore by CS Graphics

Library of Congress Cataloging-in-Publication Data
Dickerson, C. D. (Claude Douglas)
    Raw painting : the Butcher's shop by Annibale Carracci / C.D. Dickerson III.
        p. cm. — (Kimbell masterpiece series)
    Includes bibliographical references.
    ISBN 978-0-300-16640-8
1. Carracci, Annibale, 1560–1609. Butcher's shop (Kimbell Art Museum). 2. Carracci, Annibale, 1560–1609. Butcher's shop (Christ Church (University of Oxford)). 3. Carracci, Annibale, 1560–1609—Criticism and interpretation. 4. Butchers in art. 5. Kimbell Art Museum. I. Title.
    ND623.C4A62 2010
    759.5—DC22   2010021082

FRONT COVER AND FRONTISPIECE: Annibale Carracci (Italian, 1560–1609), *The Butcher's Shop* (details), c. 1582. Oil on canvas, 23½ x 28 in. (59.7 x 71 cm). Kimbell Art Museum, Fort Worth. Acquired in 1980

BACK COVER: Annibale Carracci (Italian, 1560–1609), *Self-Portrait with Other Figures*, c. 1588–90. Oil on canvas, 23⅜ x 18⅞ in. (60 x 48 cm). Pinacoteca di Brera, Milan

Contents

Fig. 1. Annibale Carracci (Italian, 1560–1609), *The Butcher's Shop*, c. 1582. Oil on canvas, 23½ x 28 in. (59.7 x 71 cm). Kimbell Art Museum, Fort Worth. Acquired in 1980

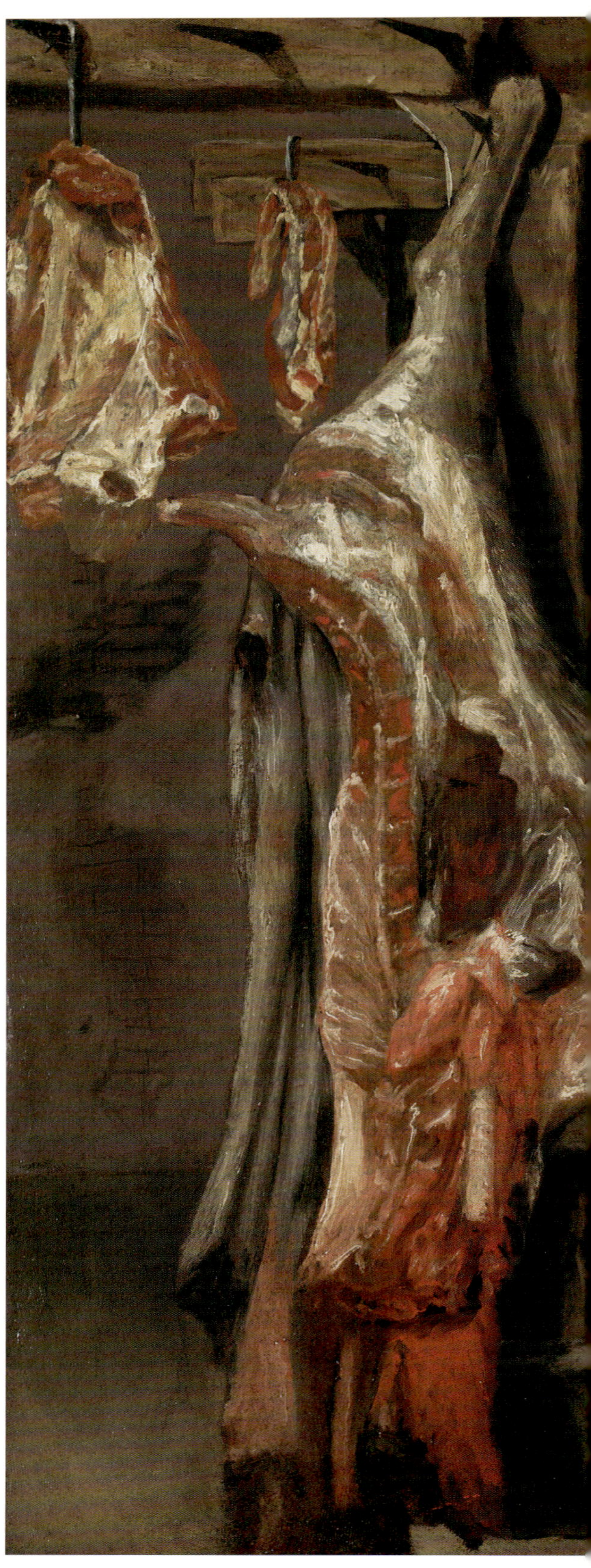

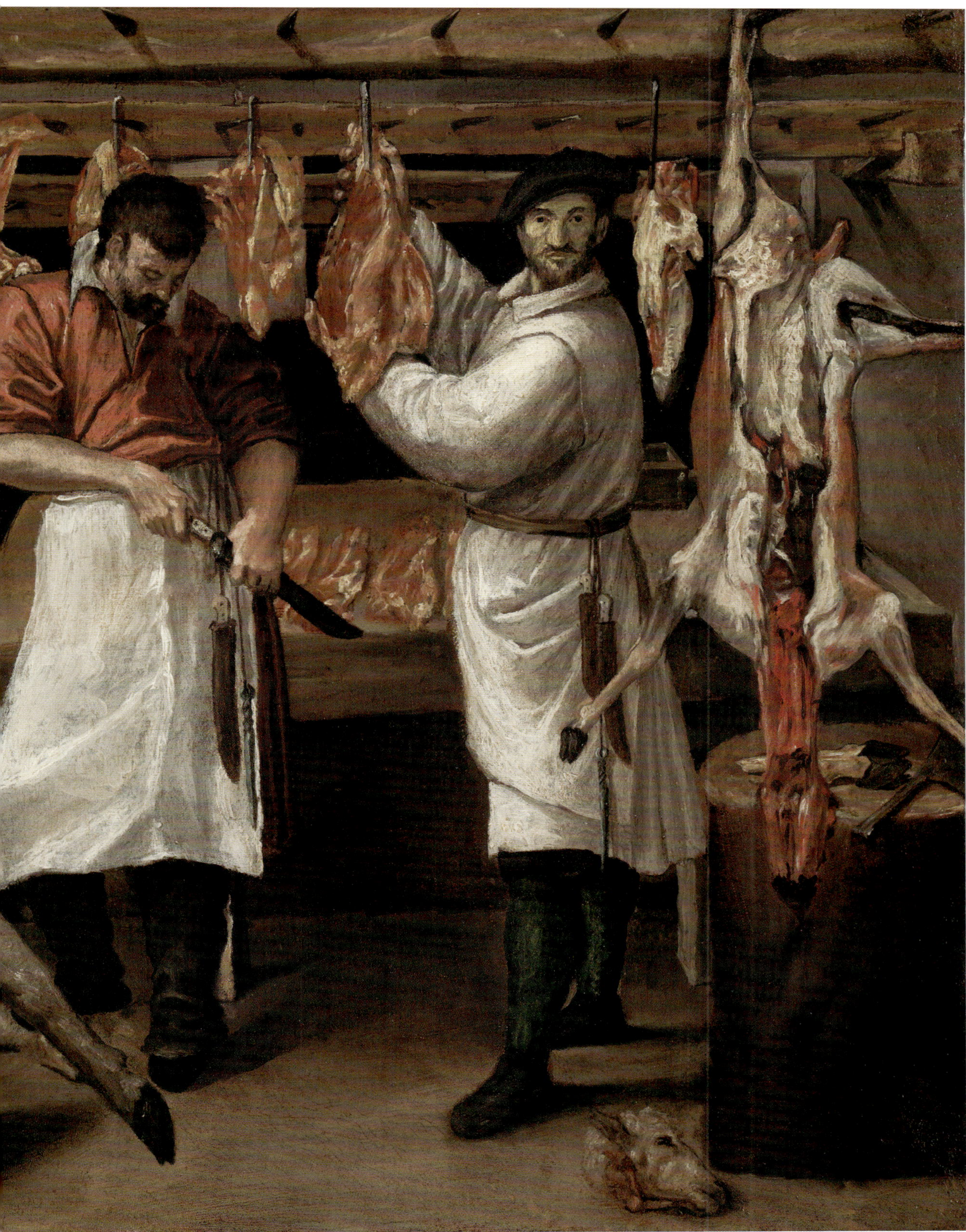

The Butcher's Shop: An Introduction

STANDING IN A SIMPLE MARKET STALL BATHED IN A SOFT, HAZY LIGHT, TWO BEARDED butchers attend to the ordinary duties of their profession (fig. 1). One grips the handle of a splaying knife and begins to pull it from its leather sheath, mustering all the concentration of an ancient priest preparing for a ritual sacrifice. His partner, on his left, is more inviting. He looks directly at us with wide eyes, as though offering the slab of meat that he is in the process of lowering from the rafter above him. Other cuts of meat, mostly veal and lamb, hang from the same beam, which is connected to a rear wall made of gray stucco over red brick. A shallow rectangular opening is cut into the wall. The butchers are partially blocked from this recess by a heavy wooden table laid out with several pieces of meat. The table is part display table, part cutting table. Another wooden beam, also studded with sharp iron spikes, marks the forward confines of the stall, and on the left is one of the wooden piers that supports this beam. The pier is almost totally concealed behind a gutted carcass of a calf, whose dissected neck and shoulder sinews are especially eye-catching for their bold, fire-engine red. Framing the butchers on the right is another gutted carcass, that of a lamb, which too hangs by a single hind leg. Evidence of slaughter exists elsewhere in the shop, as with the round chopping block in the right foreground with a butcher's cleaver and the severed leg of a hoofed animal. As our eyes move from detail to detail, we are constantly reminded of the hard and dirty work that accompanies being a butcher. The painting exudes reality, an impression strengthened by the summary quality of the brushwork. Did the young Annibale Carracci (1560–1609) not simply go to the market one morning and paint a raw transcription of butchers at work?

This book will investigate the question from multiple angles, each designed to emphasize the pictorial innovations that Annibale brought to his painting. He painted *The Butcher's Shop* in Bologna around 1582, when he was about twenty-two years old. It stands at the beginning of a stunning career during which Annibale would play a central role in the most significant revolution in Italian art since the High Renaissance. Like the other great innovator of this period, Michelangelo Merisi da Caravaggio, he sought to create a new kind of art predicated on life study. It was through genre paintings such as *The Butcher's Shop* that the young Annibale taught himself how to record the world around him in uncompromisingly real terms. Ultimately, this would be a short stop on his stylistic journey. By his mid-twenties, he had moved away from the gritty realism that characterizes *The Butcher's Shop*. But even as he advanced toward his great masterpiece, the classically themed frescoes in the Palazzo Farnese, Rome, he never completely turned his back on nature's lessons (fig. 2). His later figures, despite their considerable idealization, move and gesture with all the conviction of actual human beings.

Fig. 2. Annibale Carracci (Italian, 1560–1609), Farnese Gallery, with the central panel *The Triumph of Bacchus and Ariadne*, 1597/98–1601, fresco. Palazzo Farnese, Rome

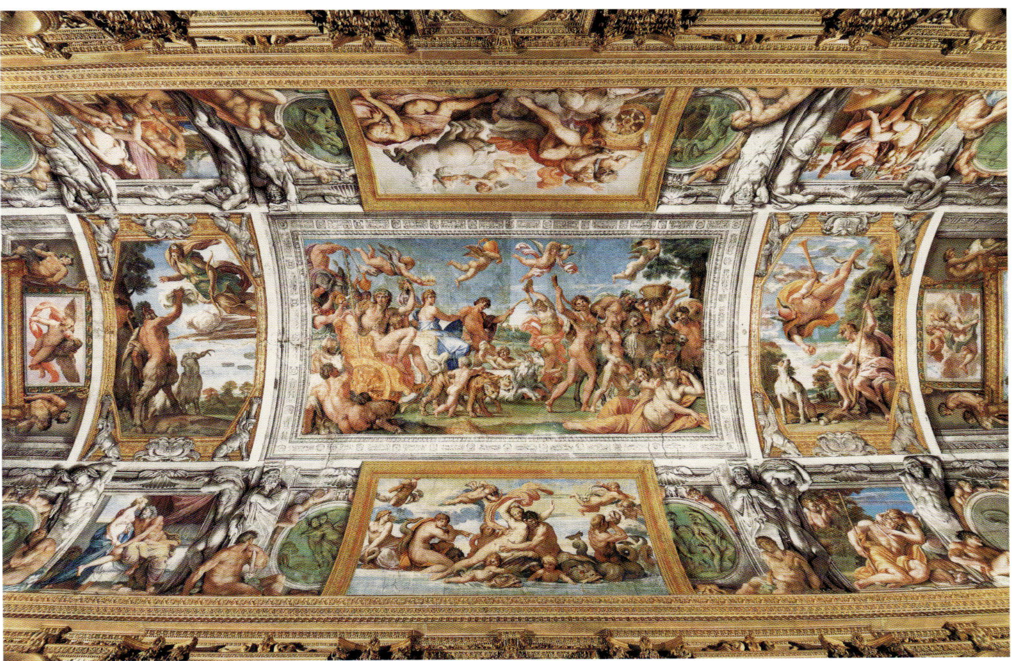

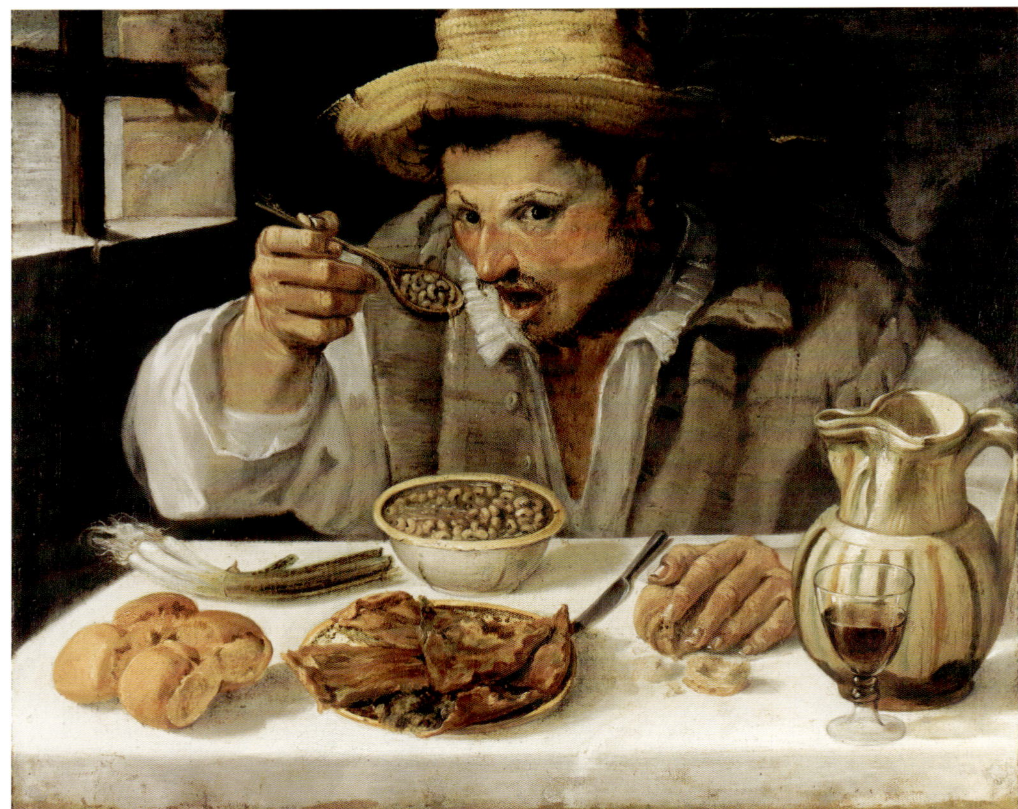

Fig. 3. Annibale Carracci (Italian, 1560–1609), *Bean Eater*, c. 1582–83. Oil on canvas, 22½ x 26¾ in. (57 x 68 cm). Galleria Colonna, Rome

Numerous paintings from Annibale's formative years—such as his famous *Bean Eater* in the Galleria Colonna, Rome (fig. 3)—document his early experiments with naturalistic painting. The Kimbell *Butcher's Shop* stands out from these, however, for the way it seems to have been executed outside his studio, in the open air, with his subjects directly before his eyes. (The French term *plein air* is often used to describe this sort of painting.) In the sixteenth century, there was no tradition of plein-air painting in Italy. The earliest records of the practice date from around 1630 and almost exclusively pertain to landscape painting. This is one of the reasons why *The Butcher's Shop* is unlikely to have been executed outdoors. Other reasons will be explored in the later chapter "The Butchers of Bologna." What is surprising is how directly observant *The Butcher's Shop* seems to be. As this book will argue, no earlier painting in Italian art makes as strong an appeal to the viewer to be regarded as an unmediated slice of life. In this respect, *The Butcher's Shop* is utterly revolutionary and shows Annibale searching for new ways to simulate in painting the visceral experience of looking at the world.

The Kimbell *Butcher's Shop* is not the only *Butcher's Shop* that Annibale painted during the early 1580s. He is responsible for a much larger treatment of the subject now in the collection of Christ Church, Oxford (fig. 6). In the next chapter, a comparison of the Kimbell and Oxford paintings will show that the Oxford *Butcher's Shop* is the more premeditated. It lacks the immediacy of the Kimbell *Butcher's Shop,* even if it exhibits many of the same pictorial innovations. From there, the book will place these innovations in art-historical context by analyzing the tradition of butcher's shop paintings in European art. The fourth chapter (pages 27–53) will view the Kimbell and Oxford paintings from the standpoint of the practical realities of being a butcher in late Renaissance Bologna. If the Kimbell *Butcher's Shop* aims to represent reality, how close to the truth does it come? The discussion will then turn to the plein-air quality of the painting and investigate its relationship to Annibale's loose painting style. The conclusion will locate the painting in Annibale's career and explore the directions his art later took.

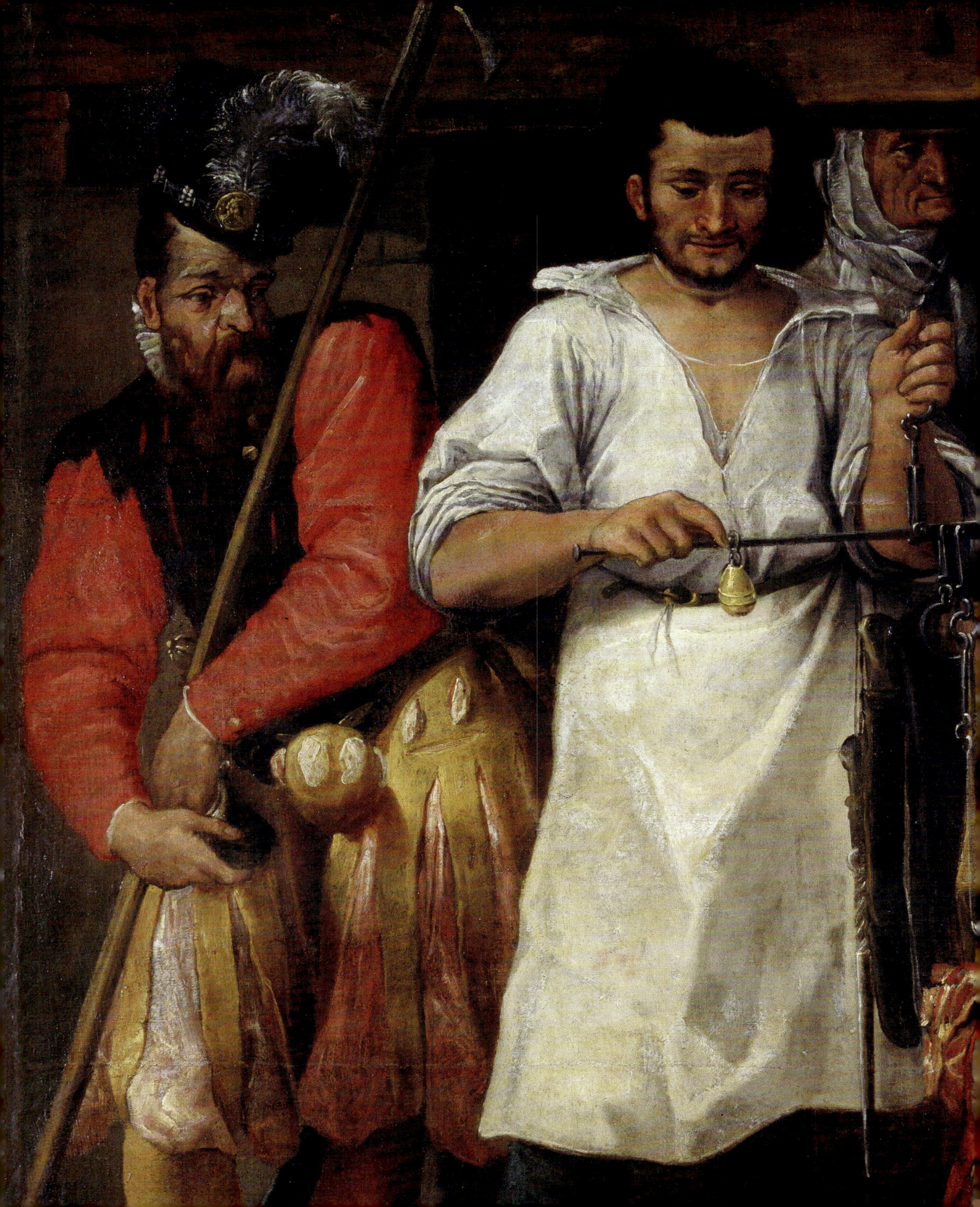

The Oxford *Butcher's Shop*

B EFORE THE KIMBELL *BUTCHER'S SHOP* CAN BE DISCUSSED WITH ANY RIGOR, IT IS FIRST necessary to introduce its much larger relative at Christ Church, Oxford (fig. 6). It came to Christ Church in 1765, a gift of the noted military leader and collector John Guise, a proud alumnus of the college.[1] Guise had likely acquired the enormous canvas from the Countess of Bristol, although it was not she who originally brought it to England. This was King Charles I, whose collection included an Italian painting of this subject when it was inventoried in 1649 for the Commonwealth Sale.[2] The connection to Charles I takes us to Italy and to one of his prime sources for pictures, the Gonzaga family of Mantua. "A large painting depicting a butcher's shop, the work of Carracci" (un quadro grande dipintovi una beccaria, oppera del Caratio) is described in their inventory of 1627, and this is almost certainly the painting now at Christ Church.[3] Where the Gonzaga acquired it—or how it made its way from Bologna to Mantua—is not known.[4] Still, the provenance is relatively complete when compared with that of the Kimbell *Butcher's Shop*, which goes back only to the early twentieth century.[5] The painting is first recorded in Haddo House, Aberdeenshire, Scotland. Its owner at the time was John Campbell Hamilton-Gordon, 7th Earl of Haddo and 1st Marquess of Aberdeen and Temair. He died in 1934, and there is no information as to whether he inherited the painting or purchased it himself. In favor of the first possibility is the fact that he is known to have inherited other notable Italian paintings from his family, including Titian's *Allegory of Prudence* (National Gallery, London).[6]

Fig. 4. Annibale Carracci, Oxford *Butcher's Shop*, detail (see fig. 6)

Something more can be said about the original owner of the Oxford *Butcher's Shop*. Because the painting is huge—nearly twelve times as large as the Kimbell *Butcher's Shop* (see fig. 5)—we can safely wager that Annibale did not produce it on speculation. It must have been a commissioned work, and the person who commissioned it must have been fairly wealthy. This is also indicated by the composition, which exhibits considerable ingenuity and must have been targeted at someone with a sound understanding of the visual arts. In other words, Annibale did not treat the painting as a casual experiment in naturalism. He was out to impress and knew that, in order to do so, he must take up certain pictorial challenges.

The principal challenge Annibale set for himself was how to arrange six figures, all engaged in meaningful activity, on a single canvas. The scene unfolds in a butcher's stall very

Fig. 5. Relative sizes of Annibale Carracci's Kimbell and Oxford *Butcher's Shop* paintings

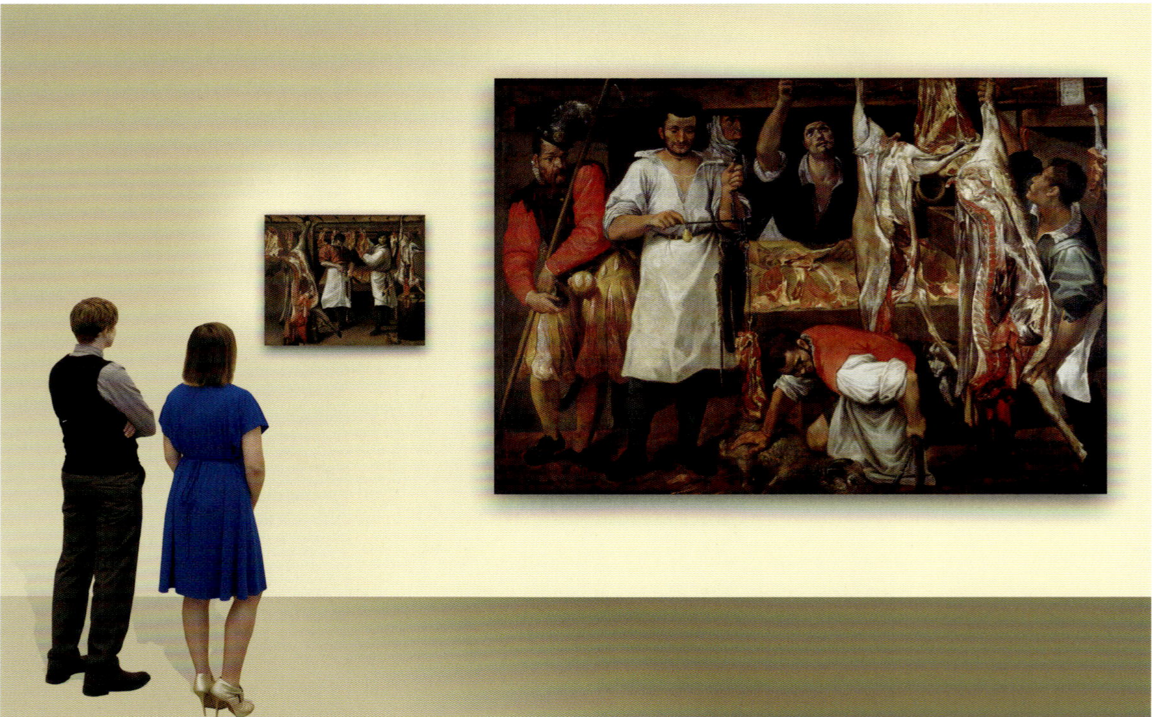

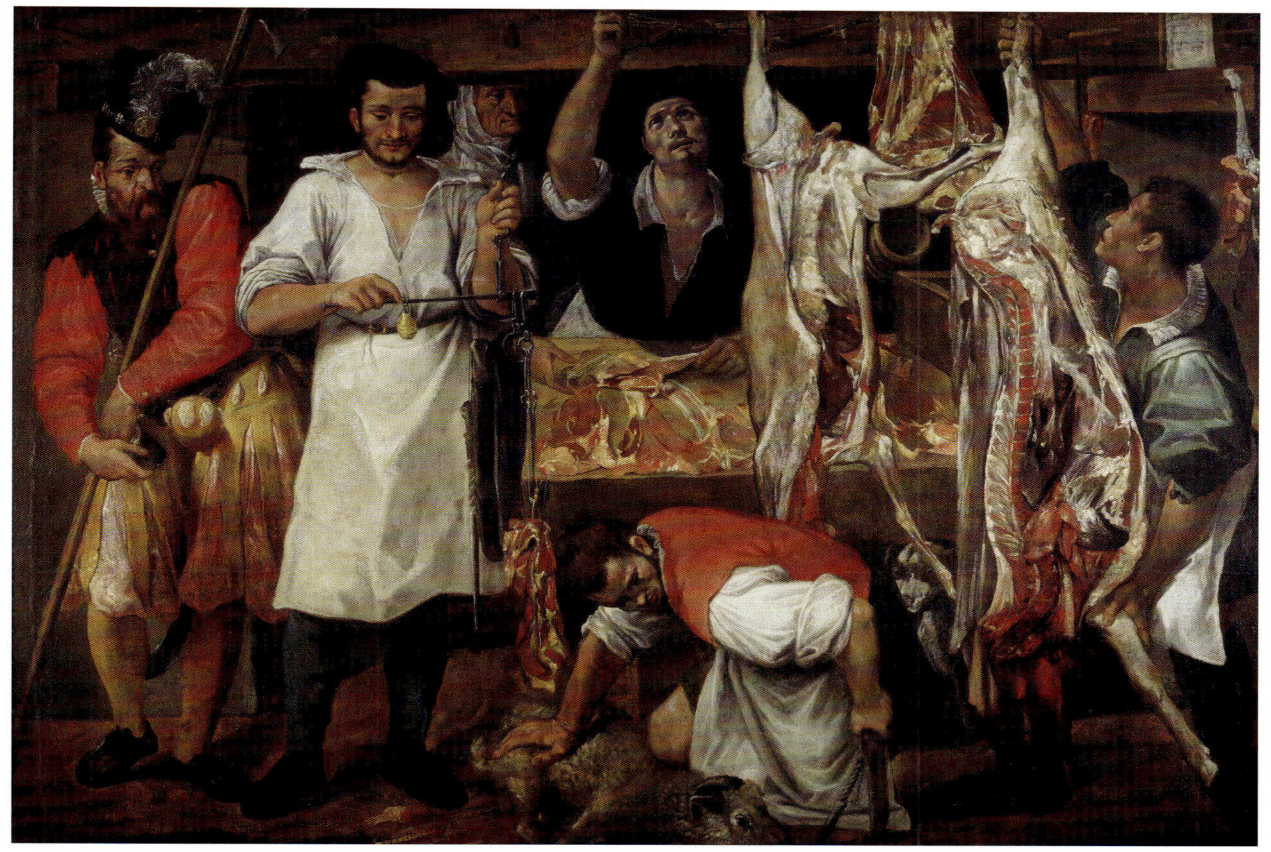

Fig. 6. Annibale Carracci (Italian, 1560–1609), *The Butcher's Shop*, c. 1582–83. Oil on canvas, 74¾ x 107⅛ in. (190 x 272 cm). Christ Church Picture Gallery, Oxford

similar to the one depicted in the Kimbell painting. A major difference, however, is that Annibale chose to populate the stall with both customers and butchers—not just butchers. The most prominent customer, dressed as a uniformed halberdier, or Swiss guard, appears on the far left. He fishes for money in his coin purse, while the butcher immediately to his left weighs a cut of meat, presumably the one that the Swiss guard is buying. In the center foreground, another butcher is at work. He is on his knees, pinning a wriggling goat that is about to be slaughtered. A third butcher, on the far right, lifts a large carcass onto an iron spike above his head. The fourth and final butcher stands in the center background behind a counter laid out with various chops. He reaches above his head for a sprig of willow, which

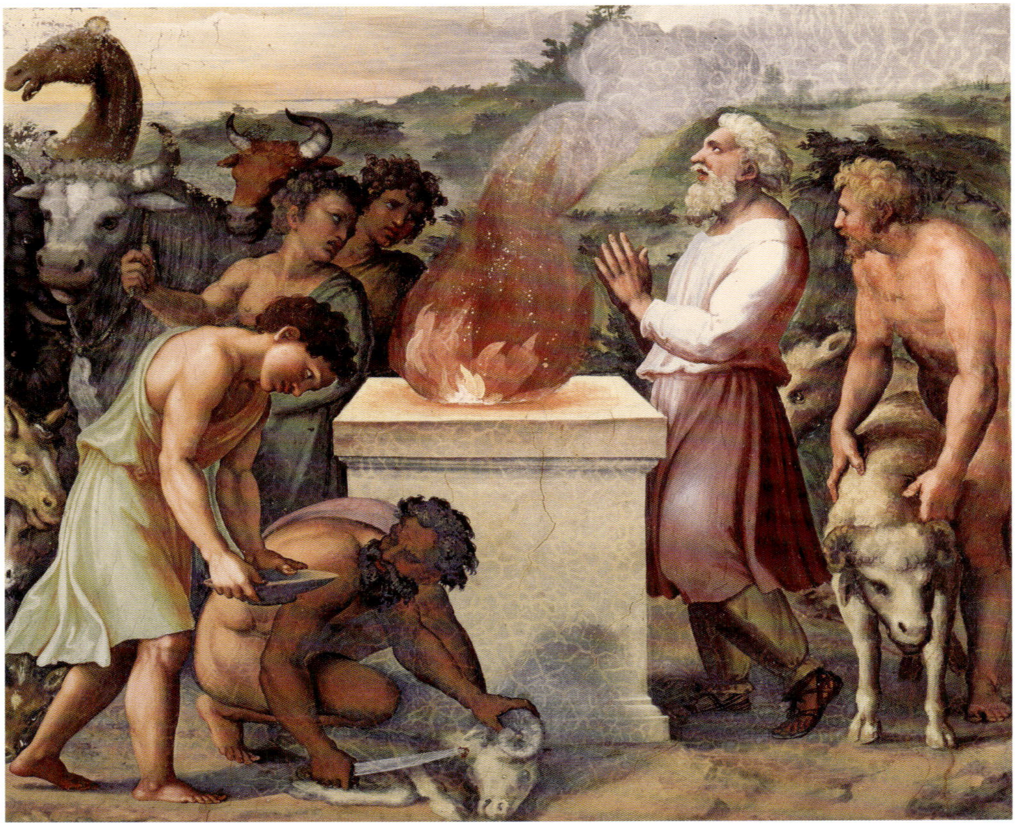

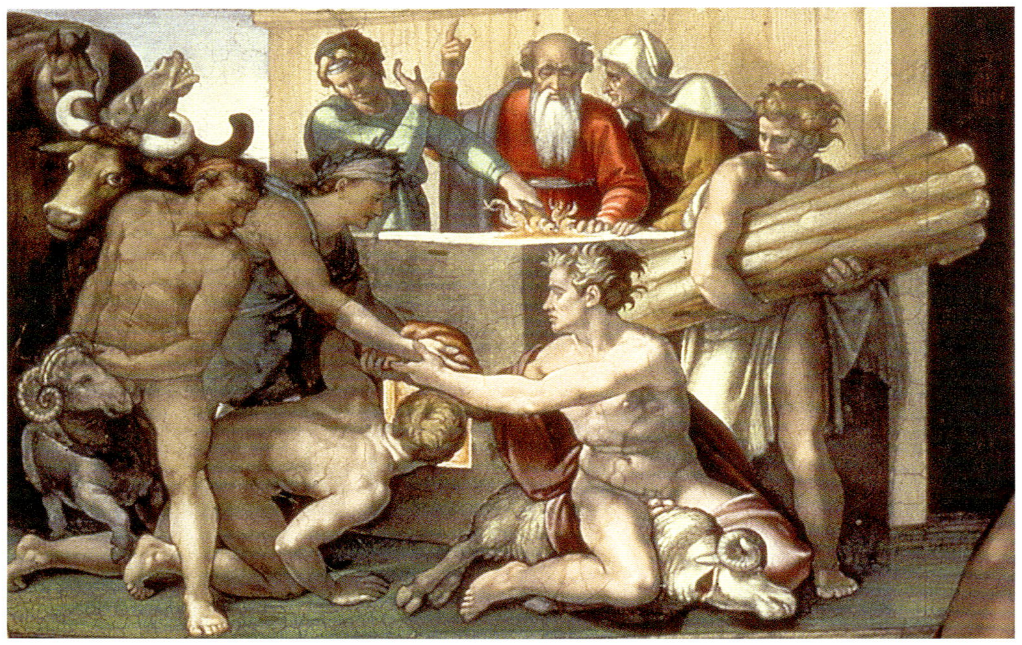

was used to wrap meat for transport at the time of the painting. He is doubtlessly attending to the second of the two customers, the old woman to his right. As if the composition were not already crowded enough, Annibale has inserted a scavenging dog (perhaps a pet) beneath the table. This raises the point that, in contrast to the Kimbell painting, there is barely any space for the figures to move. They are pushed to the edges of the canvas, and we see much less of the stall.

As demonstrated years ago by John Rupert Martin, in developing the Oxford *Butcher's Shop*, Annibale sought compositional help from two important High Renaissance paintings: Raphael's fresco of *The Sacrifice of Noah* in the Vatican Loggia (fig. 7) and Michelangelo's fresco of the same subject on the ceiling of the Sistine Chapel (fig. 8).[7] Even though Annibale had yet to travel to Rome, he could easily have studied both frescoes by way of drawn copies. In the case of the Raphael, there was also a reproductive print by Marco Dente that Annibale almost surely knew (fig. 9).[8] Between the Michelangelo and the Raphael, the latter appears to have exerted the stronger influence—or rather Annibale drew from it in more obvious ways. The kneeling butcher in the foreground is almost a mirror image of the corresponding figure in the Raphael. Annibale also looked to the Raphael for the butcher

Opposite page, top:
Fig. 7. Raphael (Italian, 1483–1520), *The Sacrifice of Noah*, 1518–19, fresco. The Loggia, Vatican Museums, Vatican City

Opposite page, bottom:
Fig. 8. Michelangelo Buonarroti (Italian, 1475–1564), *The Sacrifice of Noah*, 1508–12, fresco. Sistine Chapel, Vatican Museums, Vatican City

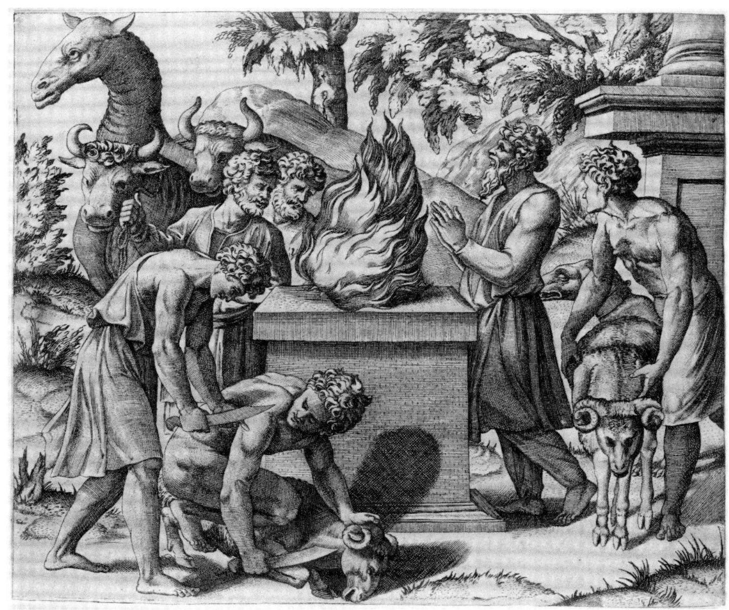

Fig. 9. Marco Dente (Italian, c. 1486–1527), *The Sacrifice of Noah*, c. 1518–27, after the fresco by Raphael (fig. 7). Engraving, 8¹⁄₁₆ x 9⁷⁄₁₆ in. (20.4 x 24 cm). The Metropolitan Museum of Art, New York. The Elisha Whittelsey Collection, The Elisha Whittelsey Fund, 1949

in profile on the right; he relates to the man with a ram, who serves a similar framing role in the fresco. Turning to the Michelangelo, the borrowings become less specific but are unquestionably present. Martin suggests that Noah was the model for the butcher with the raised hand behind the counter and that Noah's wrinkly old wife was the inspiration for the comparably aged female in the background of the painting. He also points to the man with a load of wood on the right and suggests that his pose is that of the Swiss guard in reverse. The most important contribution, however, is organizational: both the Michelangelo and the Raphael provided the basic structure for the entire painting. The flaming altar becomes the butcher's counter, while Annibale has recognized the importance of surrounding this central element with a mixture of figures seen both in profile and frontally. Not only are these borrowings exceptionally clever; they are also tinged with humor. By drawing from two canonical High Renaissance paintings of the same Old Testament sacrifice, Annibale managed to downgrade Michelangelo and Raphael to genre, while raising the everyday butcher to the level of the Bible.[9] As I will suggest later, this note of irony was intended from the outset; it was part of the larger message of the painting.

Returning to formal considerations, even if differences of scale are to be discounted between the Kimbell and Oxford butcher's shop paintings, the second is instantly the more monumental in its dependence on High Renaissance models—especially ones of such compositional stability as Raphael's and Michelangelo's frescoes of *The Sacrifice of Noah*. Annibale appears to have understood these sources so completely that we can safely assume that he prepared numerous compositional drawings in the process of arriving at his final solution for the painting. Sadly, no such sketches survive, but there is a sheet in the Royal Collection at Windsor Castle that bears studies of individual figures that were clearly preparatory for the work.[10] The more finished one corresponds to the butcher weighing meat on the left of the painting (fig. 10). He is plainly studied from life, and there is no reason to think that Annibale did not draw him on site at his stall. The same is probably true of the second drawing, which, although much sketchier, captures the basic pose of the butcher hoisting the cut of meat on the right of the canvas (fig. 11).

In many respects, the Kimbell *Butcher's Shop* is closer in spirit to these two drawings than to the Oxford *Butcher's Shop* itself. Like the Kimbell painting, the drawings seem to be informal

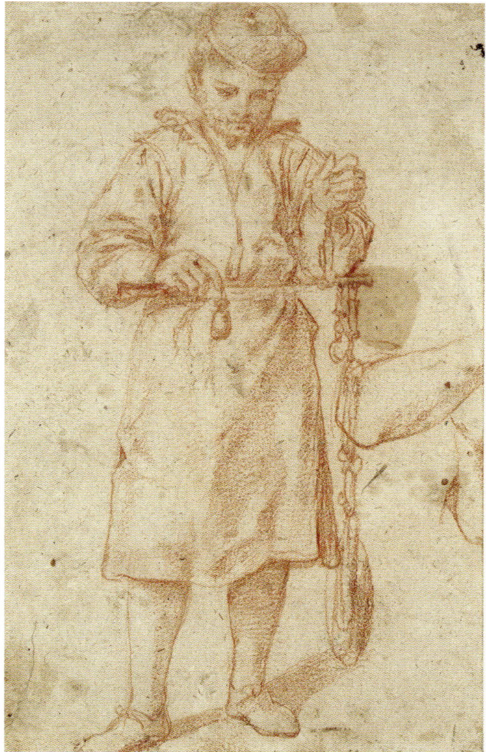

Fig. 10. Annibale Carracci (Italian, 1560–1609), *A Man Weighing Meat*, c. 1582–83. Red chalk on beige paper, 10¹⁵⁄₁₆ x 6¹¹⁄₁₆ in. (27.8 x 17 cm). The Royal Collection, Windsor Castle

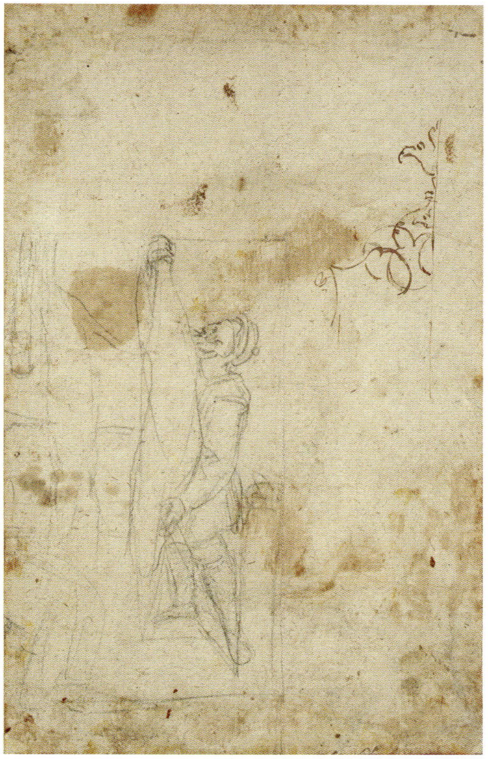

Fig. 11. Verso of fig. 10: *Butcher Hanging a Side of Meat, with a Study for an Ornament*, c. 1582–83. Black chalk with pen and brown ink

recordings of specific butchers at work. On the basis of this similarity, it has been argued that the Kimbell *Butcher's Shop* must have served as a preparatory study for the Oxford *Butcher's Shop*.¹¹ This can be neither confirmed nor denied, although if it were the case, one would surely expect the paintings to have more in common beyond mere subject matter. Admittedly, Annibale may have undertaken the Kimbell *Butcher's Shop* while thinking about the Oxford *Butcher's Shop*, in which case the Kimbell *Butcher's Shop* may have informed the Oxford painting in various preparatory ways. But there is no compelling reason to regard the paintings as precisely contemporary, and the Kimbell painting seems to me to make perfect sense as an independent genre painting, one that likely began as an informal exercise without a specific patron in mind. The one certainty is that whatever Annibale's reason for creating the Kimbell *Butcher's Shop*, he was not interested in solving complex compositional problems. He was aiming for greater casualness and thus greater believability.

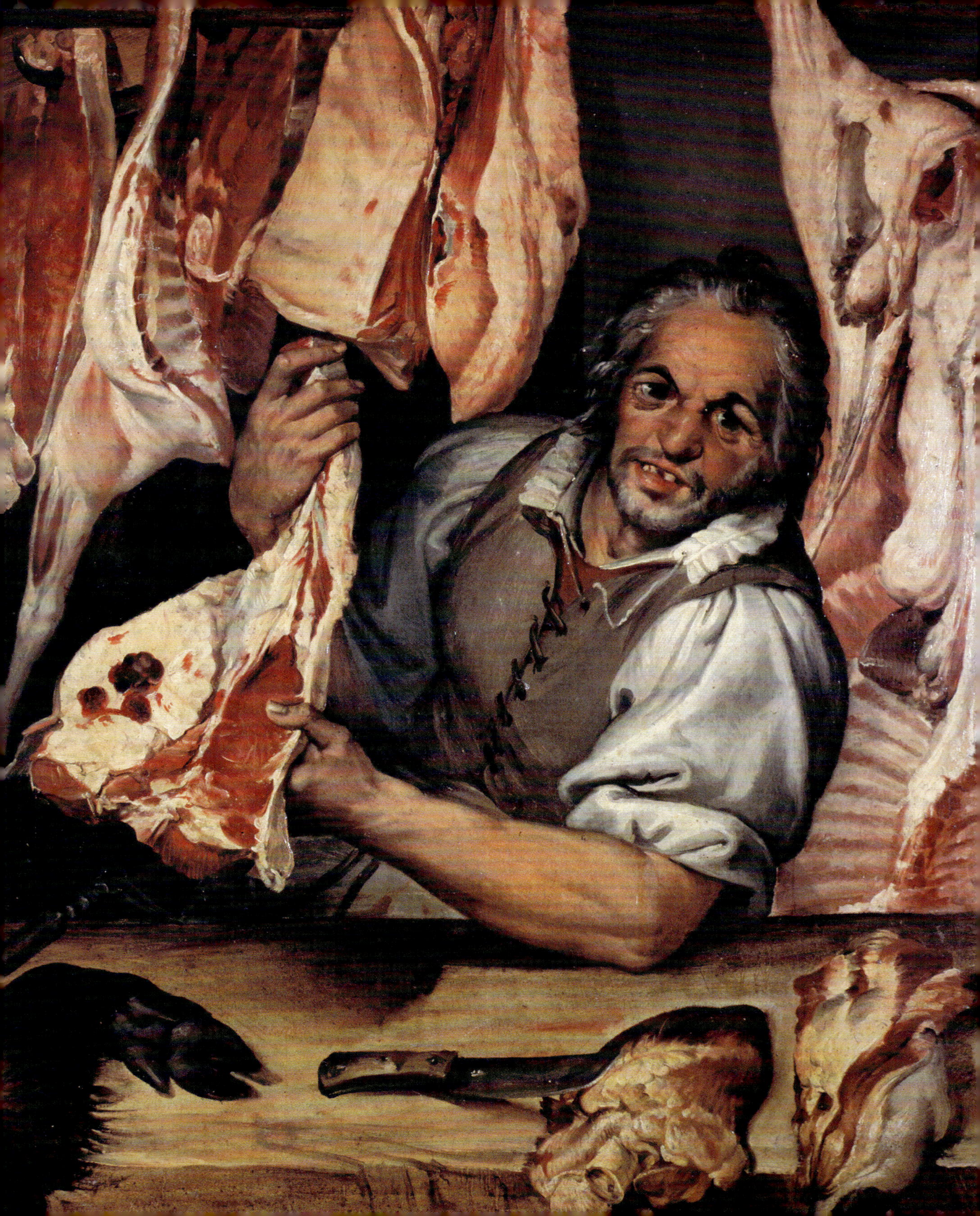

Butcher's Shop Paintings in Context

THE PREVIOUS CHAPTER EMPHASIZED THE MORE CALCULATED NATURE OF THE Oxford *Butcher's Shop*. In this chapter, we will focus on the major similarity between the two paintings, their powerful naturalism. This naturalism is clearest when they are compared to the sort of butcher's shop paintings that were being produced in northern Italy during Annibale's adolescence and early twenties.

In 1560, when Annibale was born, there was virtually no tradition in Italian painting of depicting butchers or any other kind of food vendor.[12] The tradition developed suddenly about 1580 in two northern Italian towns, Bologna and Cremona. Although Annibale must be counted as one of the pioneers of the new genre, he is unlikely to have been the first artist in northern Italy to portray a food stall in paint. That distinction is usually awarded jointly to Vincenzo Campi, from Cremona, and Bartolomeo Passarotti, from Bologna.[13] Both were significantly older than Annibale and appear to have completed their first food-vendor paintings by the time Annibale had started either of his. Campi and Passarotti took their initial inspiration from the earlier Flemish market scenes of Pieter Aertsen and Joachim Beuckelaer. Beginning about 1550, Aertsen and Beuckelaer forged a new mode of genre painting in Flanders with their large and shockingly realistic market scenes.[14] In the context of the Kimbell *Butcher's Shop*, a particularly relevant example is Aertsen's *Meat Stall* of 1551, in the North Carolina Museum of Art,

Fig. 12. Bartolomeo Passarotti, *The Butcher's Shop*, detail (see fig. 16)

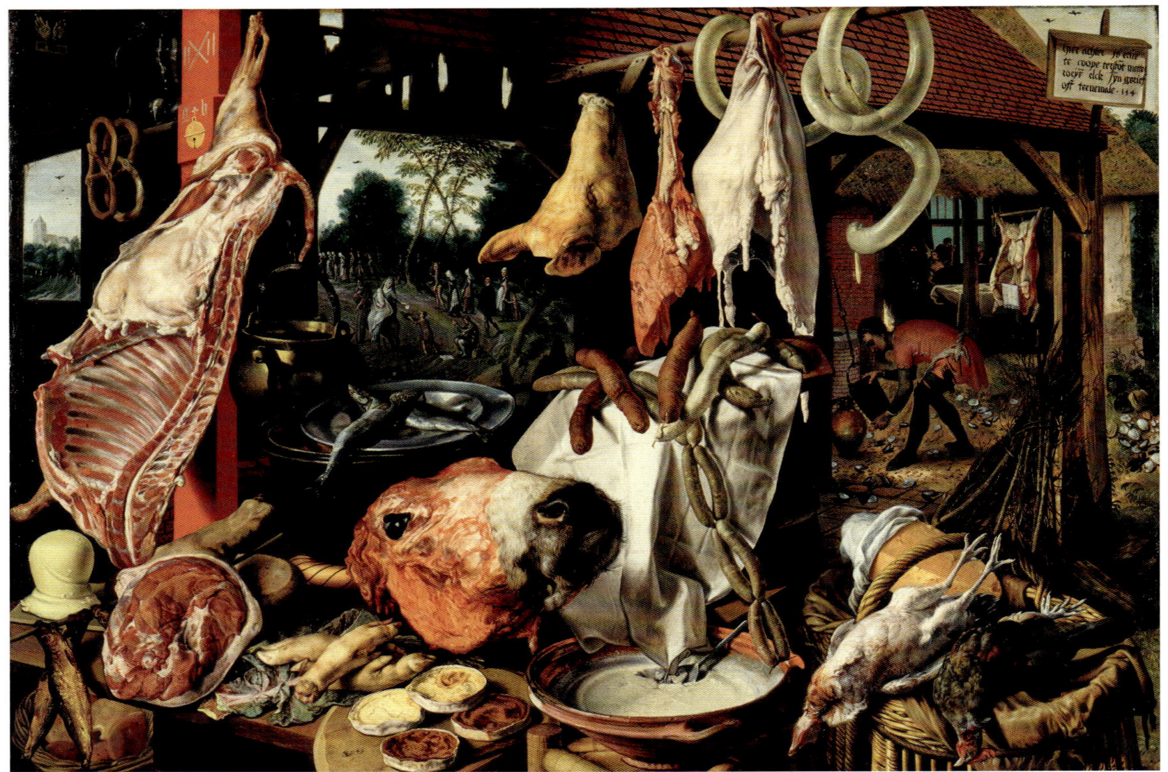

Fig. 13. Pieter Aertsen (Netherlandish, 1507/8–1575), *A Meat Stall with the Holy Family Giving Alms*, 1551. Oil on panel, 45½ x 66½ in. (115.6 x 168.9 cm). North Carolina Museum of Art, Raleigh. Purchased with funds from Wendell and Linda Murphy and various donors, by exchange

Raleigh (fig. 13). How Campi and Passarotti came to know works like the *Meat Stall* is easily explained. Some had been imported to northern Italy during the 1560s and 1570s by families like the Affaitati of Cremona, who were connected to Antwerp through their international banking business.[15] The powerful Farnese family of Parma was also an important conduit. Among the food-vendor paintings that entered their collection was Beuckelaer's large *Fish Market*, now in the Museo di Capodimonte, Naples (fig. 14).[16]

As much as Campi or Passarotti may have been impressed by Aertsen's and Beuckelaer's market scenes, they altered their Flemish prototypes in several fundamental ways. First, where the northern paintings often include religious references in their backgrounds (as with the scene of the Flight into Egypt in the background of Aertsen's *Meat Stall*), the Italian paintings are devoid of overt religious meaning.[17] The second important deviation from the Flemish models is stylistic. Campi's *Fish Vendors* in the Pinacoteca di Brera, Milan, offers a useful comparison (fig. 15).[18] It is one of five food-vendor paintings that Campi painted around 1580 for an unknown Cremonese patron. In contrast to Beuckelaer's earlier *Fish Market*, Campi's painting strikes a much less veristic chord. The composition is more rigid, and the figures' gestures and interactions are more exaggerated. These are not the earnest merchants of Beuckelaer's painting but comedic, low-life types. It is hard not to smile, for instance, at the happy couple on the far left who stuff their mouths with beans.

We shall return to that couple, but before doing so, it is instructive to look at another of the earliest food-vendor paintings produced in northern Italy, Passarotti's famous *Butcher's*

Fig. 14. Joachim Beuckelaer (Flemish, c. 1533–1574), *Fish Market*, 1569–70. Oil on panel, 61⅜ x 83⅞ in. (156 x 213 cm). Museo Nazionale di Capodimonte, Naples

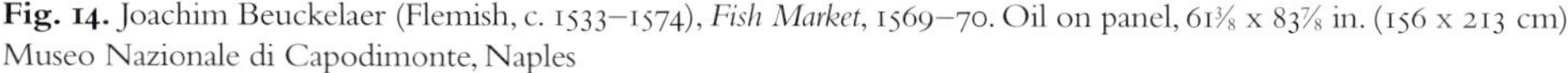

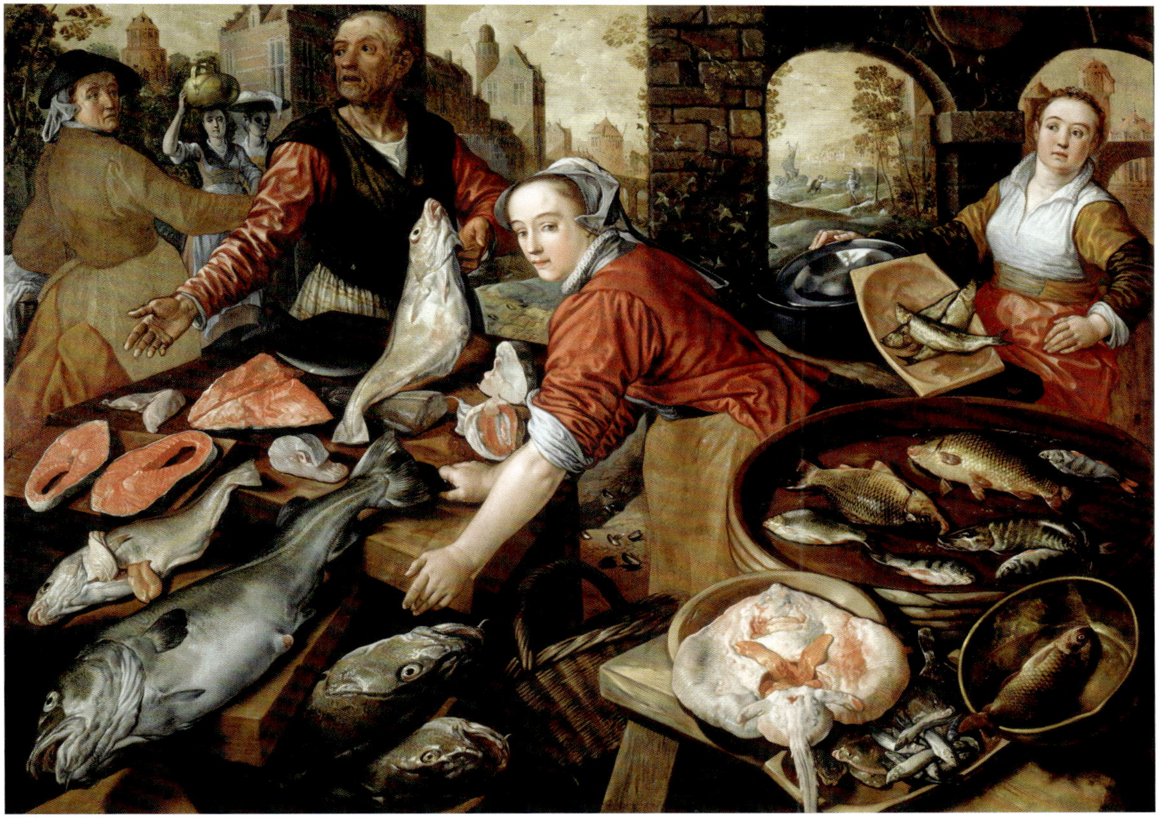

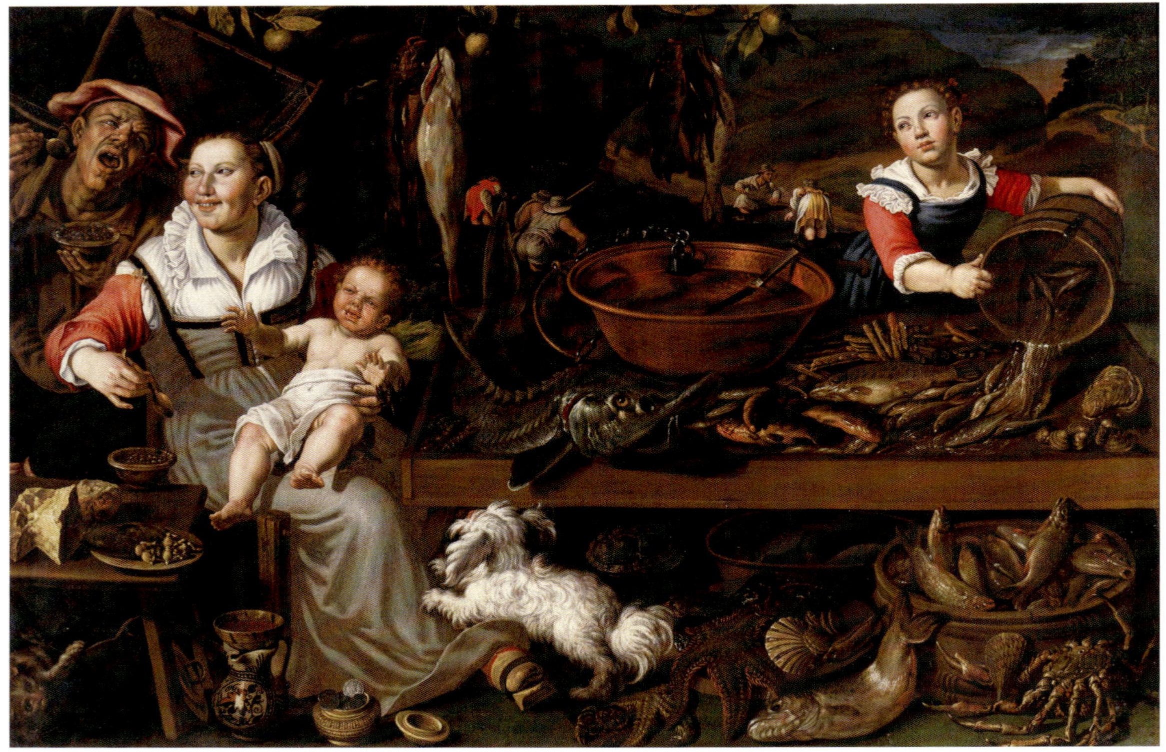

Fig. 15. Vincenzo Campi (Italian, c. 1530–1591), *Fish Vendors*, c. 1580. Oil on canvas, 57⅛ x 84⅝ in. (145 x 215 cm). Pinacoteca di Brera, Milan

Shop in the Galleria Nazionale d'Arte Antica, Rome (fig. 16). It was likely painted about 1580, and there seems a high probability that Annibale had studied it prior to undertaking his own butcher's shop paintings.[19] Not only was Passarotti the leading artist in Bologna during Annibale's formative years, but there are also indications that, as a teenager, Annibale may have spent a short stint in the older artist's studio.[20] His apprenticeship could have happened anytime between about 1575 and 1580. Passarotti's approach to market scenes was very similar to Campi's, although Passarotti tended to be less strongly wedded to the Flemish precedents of Aertsen and Beuckelaer. His figures, as demonstrated by the two butchers in his Rome *Butcher's Shop*, are more emphatically comedic. With their sly smiles and roguish looks, they seem to be asking the viewer not to think about the hard work, blood, and guts that accompany being a butcher. This lends the whole scene an air of fantasy, even if many of the individual details are painted with a high degree of realism. The disjunction is likely born of the fact that Passarotti has approached the painting as though he were directing a burlesque play. He has chosen two stock low-life characters, placed them on a simple stage, and surrounded them with various realistic props. Indeed, contemporary theater was almost certainly an influence on Passarotti.[21] He had undoubtedly seen *commedia dell'arte* performances, full of actors playing silly, lower-class roles, and there were many other kinds of bawdy, comedic theater that were popular in Bologna during the sixteenth century. It is difficult to connect any of his paintings to a specific play; the connection is of a more

Fig. 16. Bartolomeo Passarotti (Italian, 1529–1592), *The Butcher's Shop*, c. 1577–80. Oil on canvas, 44⅛ x 59⅞ in. (112 x 152 cm). Galleria Nazionale d'Arte Antica, Palazzo Barberini, Rome

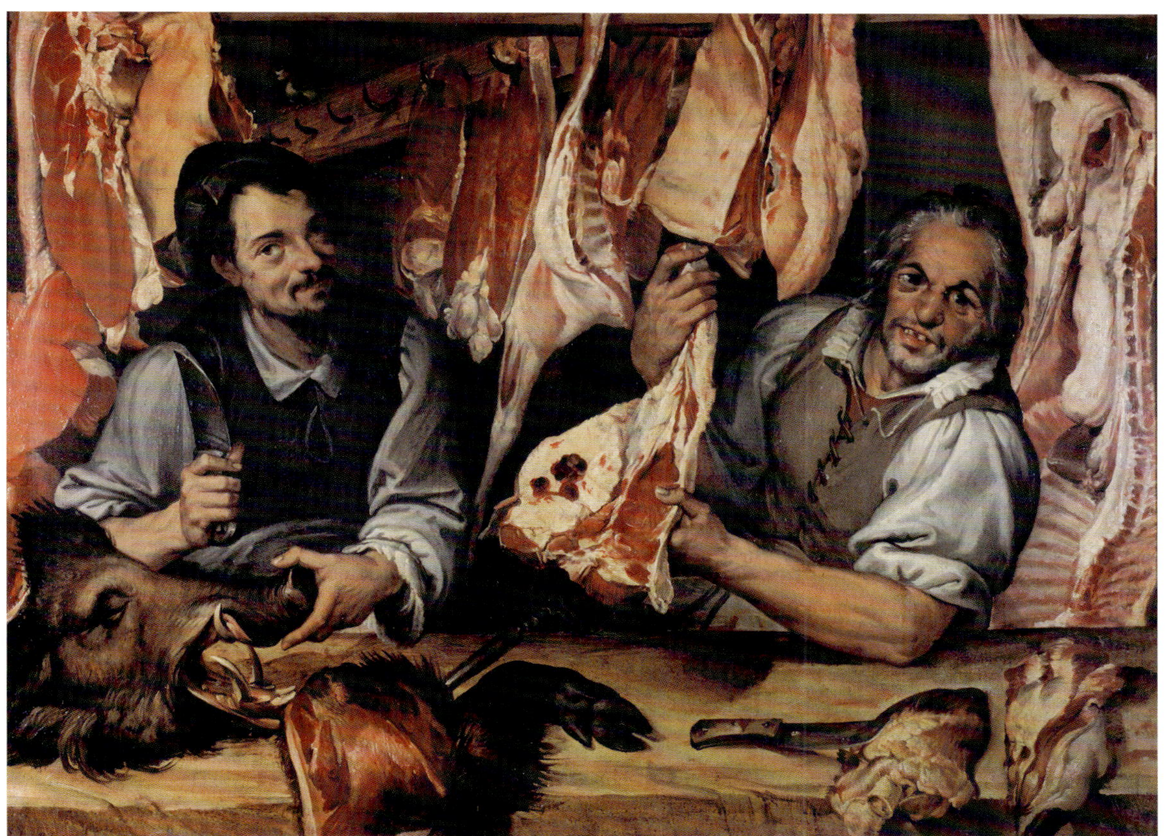

general, visual kind. Owing to its naturalistic portrayals and suggested engagement with a real audience, Passarotti's *Butcher's Shop* conveys much of the immediacy of a live burlesque performance. But this is not to suggest that a viewer of the time would have mistaken the painting for an exact transcription of reality. It presents a fiction, like any piece of theater.

If Campi's and Passarotti's market scenes are truly fictitious, what story are they trying to tell? No answer is possible without first considering their comedic aspects.[22] These are not objective portrayals of low life directed at "low" people. The audience was a high one, and the portrayals were meant to emphasize the stereotypical vulgarity of social inferiors. The viewer was invited not to sympathize with low people but to laugh at them and, through laughter, to take comfort in the fact that he or she was naturally superior.

Recently, Sheila McTighe has demonstrated that comedy is only the broadest cultural context in which these paintings can be placed.[23] They reflect several contemporary discourses. The first (and perhaps most relevant) is the debate over the suitability of different foods for different social classes. This topic began to grip the minds of various northern Italian thinkers during the 1570s.[24] What began as a quest to understand the nature of foods resulted in a more sweeping theory about which foods were right for which social levels. Rough and hard foods such as beans and scallions were thought to be appropriate only for low people, while poultry and fish, considered the noblest foods, were to be reserved for the elite. Campi's *Fish Vendors* appears to rely on many of these notions for its imagery.[25] The peasants on the left pay no attention to the fish because it is not appropriate for them. Their food is beans, which they happily devour. The only time that peasants were supposed to come into contact with fish was during its harvesting, and this is precisely how the other peasants in the painting are depicted. It is also possible to see Passarotti's *Butcher's Shop* as a response to the food debate.[26] Red meat was thought to be difficult to digest and thus appropriate only for the crude biologies of manual laborers such as butchers. Paintings such as Passarotti's seem to reflect this belief by suggesting that the people who eat, touch, and sell crude meat are just as crude as the meat itself, both in appearance and character.

Two additional discourses can be brought to bear on Passarotti's and Campi's market scenes. The first centers on proverbs, and the second is the growing fascination with scientific displays of natural wonders. Regarding proverbs, short popular sayings that expressed some commonplace truth had long been an integral part of Italian literary culture, but it was not until the sixteenth century that they began to be studied as a genre in their own right. Gentleman scholars, or *virtuosi*, prepared collections of proverbs for publication, and the upper classes took increasing delight in contemplating the peculiar folksy wisdom that resided within them. Many motifs in Passarotti's and Campi's market scenes can be directly linked to known proverbs. In Campi's *Fish Vendors*, for instance, the peasant woman emptying a bucket of small fish, or sardines, likely illustrates the popular adage "women and sardines are better small" (donne e sardine, son buone piccoline).[27] In some of their later food-vendor paintings, Campi and Passarotti went to considerable lengths to string multiple proverbs together to convey larger and more complex moralizing messages. Viewers with the right education would have tried to "solve" these paintings like a game.

Similar sophistication would have been needed to appreciate the influence of the natural sciences on the earliest food-vendor paintings.[28] Just at the time Campi and Passarotti were breaking into the genre, the study of nature was gaining in rigor, and one preoccupation was with the cataloguing of natural specimens. Naturalists—including the preeminent one in Italy, Ulisse Aldrovandi of Bologna—took great pains to collect specimens of flora and fauna and to display them in systematic arrangements.[29] The arrangements were often housed in dedicated rooms known as chambers of arts and wonders, or *Kunst- und Wunderkammern*.[30] A famous illustration of one such chamber dates from 1599 and is that of the Neapolitan naturalist Ferrante Imperato (fig. 17).[31] The display of marine animals on the ceiling can be likened to the careful groupings of fish that Campi presents in his *Fish Vendors*, where different species are carefully separated into buckets and individual specimens rendered with scientific precision. Given that some of these paintings are known to have gone to patrons who appear to have been active naturalists themselves and had formed their own *Kunstkammern*—such as the wealthy Hans Fugger of Augsburg, in southern Germany—it seems likely that Campi and Passarotti were not ignorant of the *kunstkammer* phenomenon and tailored their food-vendor paintings to appeal to the same kind of taste and interest.[32]

This digression into the state of genre painting in northern Italy around 1580 has been intended to make one major point: that the immediate precedents in Italian art for the

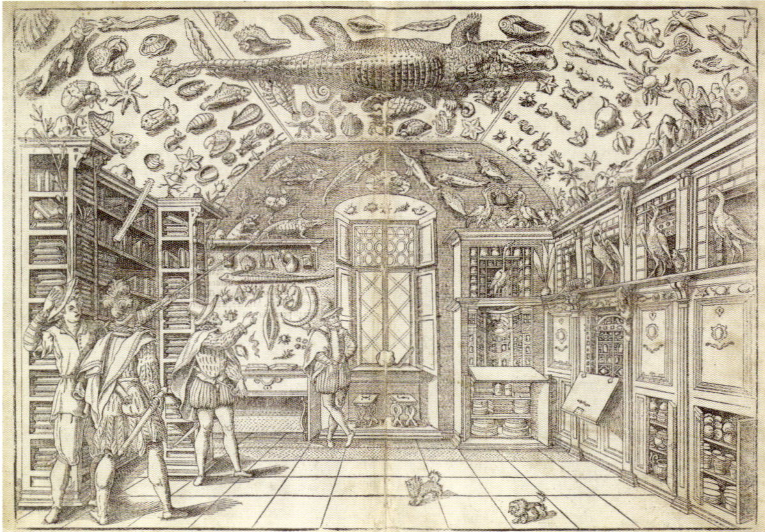

Kimbell *Butcher's Shop* were born of complicated motives, not the simple desire on the part of artists to record real butchers or other food vendors at work. They bear, albeit to differing degrees, a pronounced artificiality—or, as is often said, they look comic—and this is where the Kimbell *Butcher's Shop* breaks with tradition. Its figures convey an earnestness that is worlds away from the butchers of Passarotti, who gesture and glance with all the contrivances of ham actors on a stage. Annibale adhered to a much simpler formula, not pretending to be a theater director who must dress up his actors to play the role of butchers. His butchers are who they are.

The same is not strictly true of the Oxford *Butcher's Shop*. Yes, the four butchers are conceived in a monumental and impressively naturalistic style, but what of the uniformed halberdier on the left and the old woman in the far background? They stand out for their clumsy actions (the halberdier twists awkwardly to reach past his codpiece into his purse) and exaggerated features (the old woman casts a glacial stare, and her face is deeply incised with wrinkles). Annibale even seems to have painted these figures in a more schematic manner to emphasize that we are not to group them with the honest and hardworking butchers who are the focus of the painting.[33] If they belong anywhere, it is in the world of comedy. Indeed, the Oxford *Butcher's Shop* is not totally unlike Campi's and Passarotti's food-vendor paintings. Like them, it makes use of stock literary characters and social types—the plodding government official, the nagging hag—and seems to rely on satire to convey a larger message. This message likely hinges on the fact that both figures play the role of customers in the scene, suggesting that there is a socioeconomic point to be gleaned. In the next chapter, which deals with the butcher's trade in late Renaissance Bologna, we will inquire into what this point may be. For now, it may be noted that in developing his largest and most complex market scene, Annibale was not totally blind to the comedic approach of his older colleagues, Campi and Passarotti. As evidenced by his treatment of the halberdier and the old woman, he was happy to relax his naturalistic standards for the sake of competing with these veterans. Indeed, he may have felt pressure from his patron—whoever the patron might have been—to conform.

Still, Annibale was Annibale, and being different was who he was. The Oxford *Butcher's Shop* is unlike anything by Campi or Passarotti for the simple reason that only two of its figures—not all of them—are comedic. The four butchers who dominate the composition invite the viewer's respect, and this is a direct consequence of the naturalistic approach that Annibale took in painting them. Each of the four is expertly studied, and we have already seen that preparatory drawings, almost certainly done from life, played a role. In developing his figures, Annibale would have not only studied actual butchers at work but also drawn from live models posed in his studio. Of the four butchers in the Oxford *Butcher's Shop*, the one in the foreground on his knees strikes the most comfortable pose and could well be a studio model (fig. 18). Indeed, it has been demonstrated that, only a year or two later, Annibale employed a studio model for a very similar kneeling man in one of his frescoes in the Palazzo Fava, Bologna (fig. 19).[34]

The benefits of life study were clear to Annibale from the outset of his career, and he was keen to exploit them whenever he could, which was practically always.[35] This set him apart from nearly all his colleagues in Bologna, who continued to favor the prevailing style of art practiced in central Italy, now commonly known as Mannerism. To gain a clearer understanding of Mannerism, it is helpful to think of the Mannerist artist closest to Annibale,

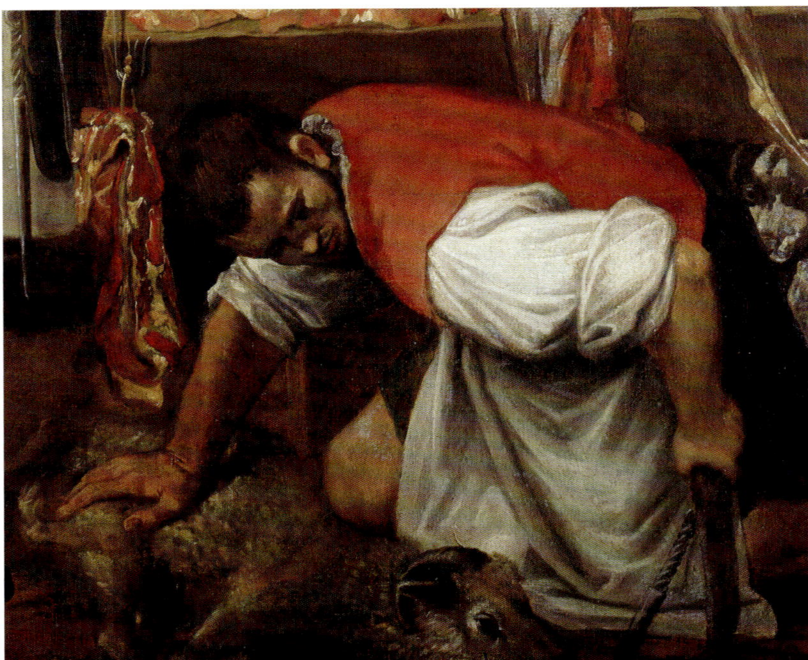

Fig. 18. Annibale Carracci, Oxford *Butcher's Shop*, detail (see fig. 6)

the older Passarotti. When Passarotti painted his butchers, he did not study real butchers on the streets but recorded what he saw in his mind's eye, and the consequence is that his butchers look unashamedly artificial. This becomes abundantly clear when we focus on the proud and individualized faces that Annibale has given to the four butchers in his Oxford *Butcher's Shop*. They are in no way cartoonish like Passarotti's but have qualities more typical of actual portraits. Their features are sharp; their hairstyles differ; and their expressions are calm and thoughtful.

In the Kimbell *Butcher's Shop*, there is less specificity in the faces owing to the reduced scale of the painting. But there can be no mistaking that these butcher-figures also reflect specific human beings. If we had any doubts, Annibale has reassured us by giving them an utterly realistic space in which to operate. Note the wealth of naturalistic details, from the shadows coming off the iron spikes overhead to the deteriorating stucco on the left wall. Ultimately, there is practically nothing in this painting that leaps out at us as being odd or

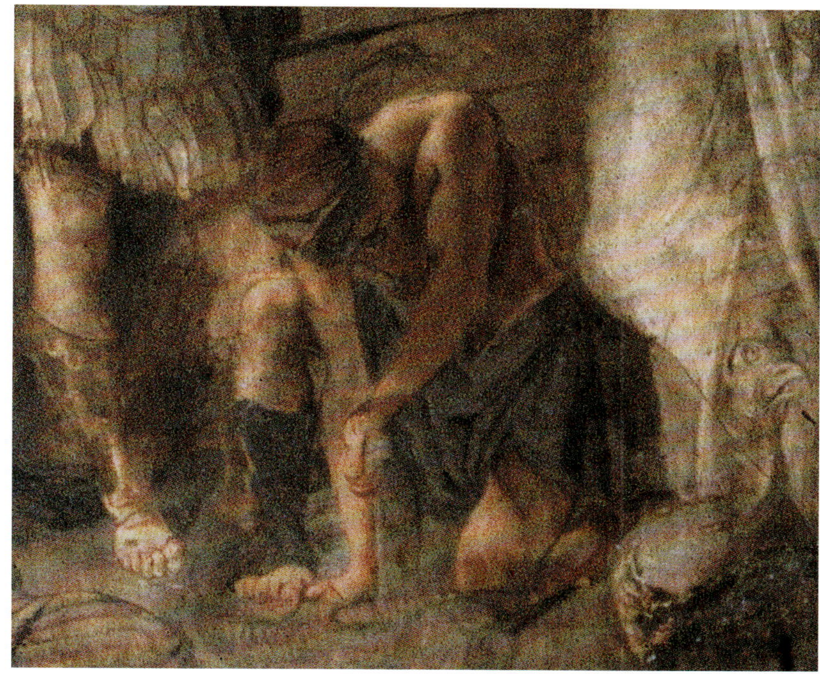

Fig. 19. Annibale Carracci (Italian, 1560–1609), *The Building of the Argo* (detail), 1584, fresco. Sala di Giasone, Palazzo Fava, Bologna

fabricated or that might make us contemplate secondary meanings. Perhaps the only instance in which we may hesitate is with the butcher on the left, whose pose—the arm akimbo; the elegant drawing of his weapon; the crisp, white linen; and the solemn demeanor—seems more appropriate for an aristocratic portrait than a "snapshot."[36] Even so, the illusion of reality is hardly shattered, and it is on the strength of this illusion that the Kimbell *Butcher's Shop* stands so far outside the mainstream. Unlike the Oxford *Butcher's Shop*, which is more contrived, with its formal poses and laughable halberdier and old woman, the Kimbell painting aims for total naturalness. We are meant to think that we are glimpsing a slice of everyday life. But are we? To claim that the Kimbell *Butcher's Shop* is revolutionary for its naturalism is not necessarily to claim that it presents an exact transcription of reality in the way a candid photograph does. Annibale may have taken certain liberties, and one way to check for these liberties is to inquire into the practical realities of being a butcher in Bologna during Annibale's lifetime, the subject of the next chapter.

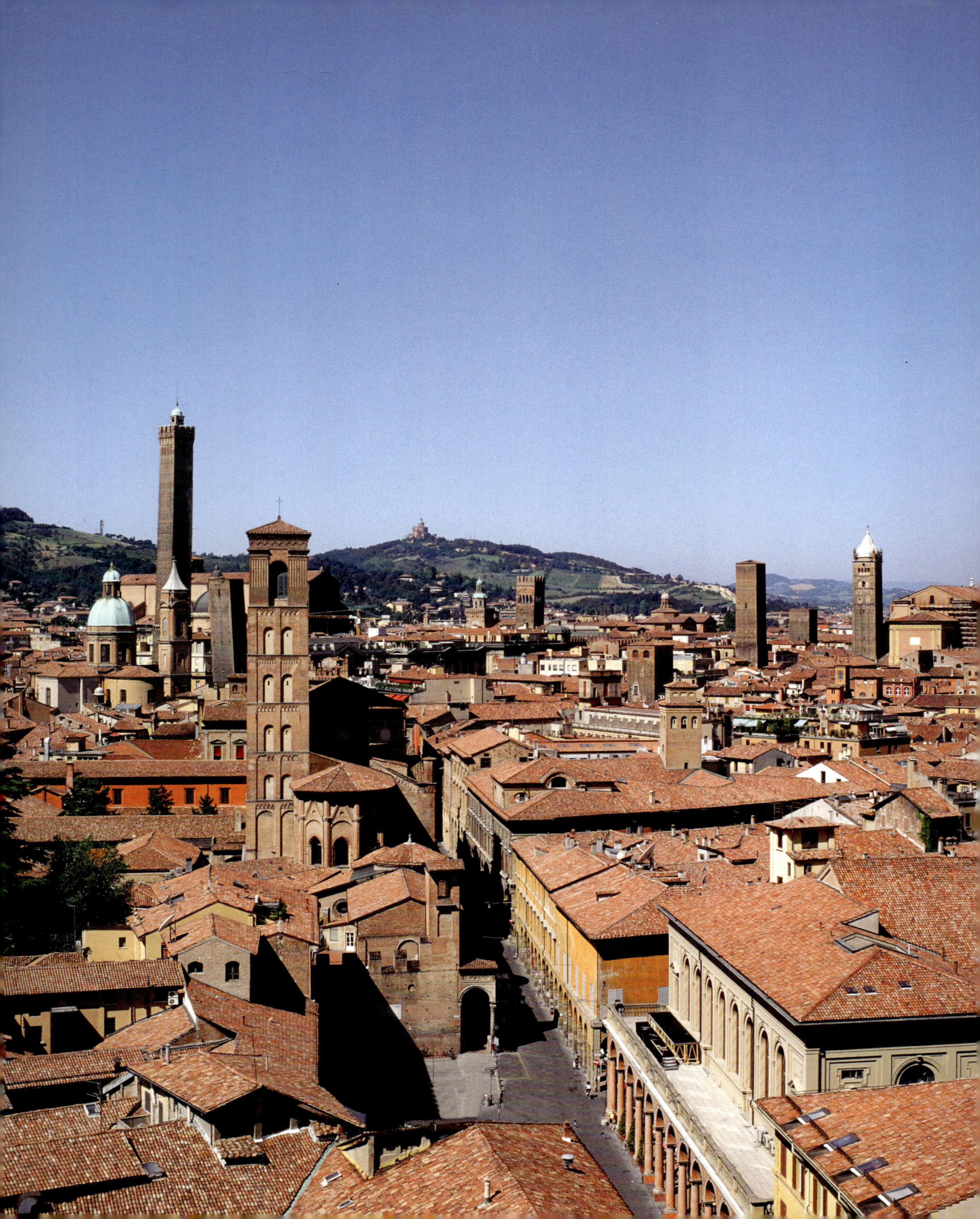

The Butchers of Bologna

I N THE YEAR ANNIBALE WAS BORN, 1560, BOLOGNA WAS A PROSPEROUS CITY APPROACHING sixty thousand inhabitants.[37] It was blessed with a sound economy, a stable government, one of the oldest and largest universities in Europe, and a thriving religious community. Within its medieval walls, and beneath its famous skyline of medieval towers (fig. 20), a wide range of professions, both intellectual and manual, were represented. Nearly a quarter of the population was connected to the silk trade, Bologna's largest industry. Paper and plain-woven cotton ranked second and third. Not surprisingly, it was the patrician class that reaped the greatest rewards from the economy, and it also played a major role in the government. From 1506, and continuing well after Annibale's death in 1609, Bologna was part of the Papal States and governed by a senate comprised of noblemen and a legate appointed by the pope. The seat of government was the Palazzo Comunale, located on the magisterial Piazza Maggiore (fig. 21). Nearby was the Palazzo del Archiginnasio, which dates from the early 1560s and was built to house the university, whose departments had heretofore been scattered in various buildings across the city (fig. 22). Because of the university, Bologna boasted a far more sophisticated population than many Italian cities. It was home to foreign and local students, professors of law, medicine, and other fields, and important scholars. Another group that contributed to the intellectual life of the city were the ecclesiastics, whose ranks were unusually strong and devoted because of Cardinal Gabriele Paleotti. A native Bolognese who returned as bishop in 1567, Paleotti was committed to making Bologna the

Fig. 20. View of Bologna from the Torre della Specola, looking southwest

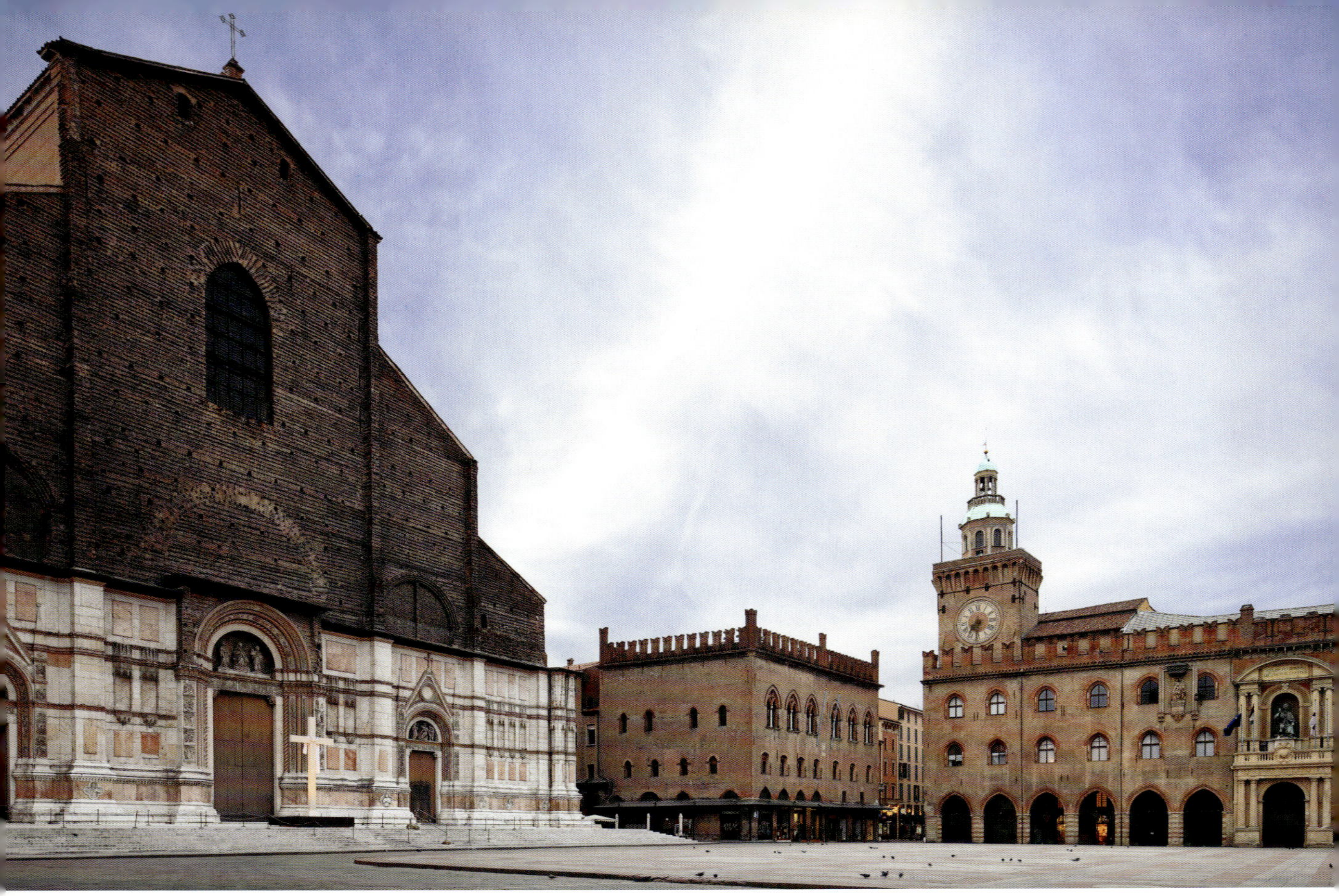

Fig. 21. Piazza Maggiore, Bologna, with the Basilica of San Petronio (left) and the Palazzo Comunale (right)

Fig. 22. Antonio Terribilia
(Italian 1500/1508–1568),
Palazzo del Archiginnasio,
Bologna, 1562–63

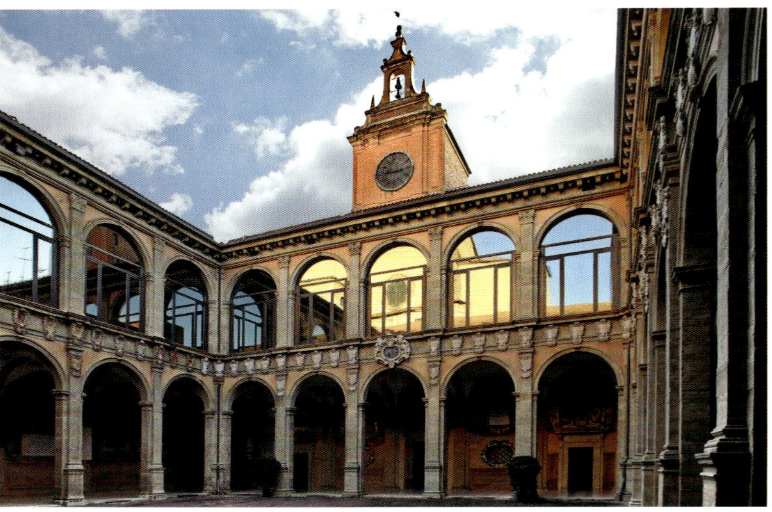

model Catholic city. His zeal for reform stirred a new fervor and led to the founding of many religious institutions. This ensured an expanding pool of well-educated clergy.

Like any modern city, however, Bologna would have been nothing without an efficient supply of food. Located on the southern edge of the great Po Valley, it was surrounded on three sides by highly fertile fields; to the south rose the Apennines, whose forests brought their own edible riches (fig. 23). The farmers who cultivated the lands around Bologna were the foundation of the food economy. Their wheat, livestock, and produce kept Bologna fed. The financial well-being of the farmers depended on their ability to deliver their products efficiently to the nearby city, and Bologna was like any urban center in having a portion of its economy devoted to food preparation and distribution. Livestock and agricultural products reached the mouths of average city dwellers only after passing through numerous

Fig. 23. Map of northern Italy

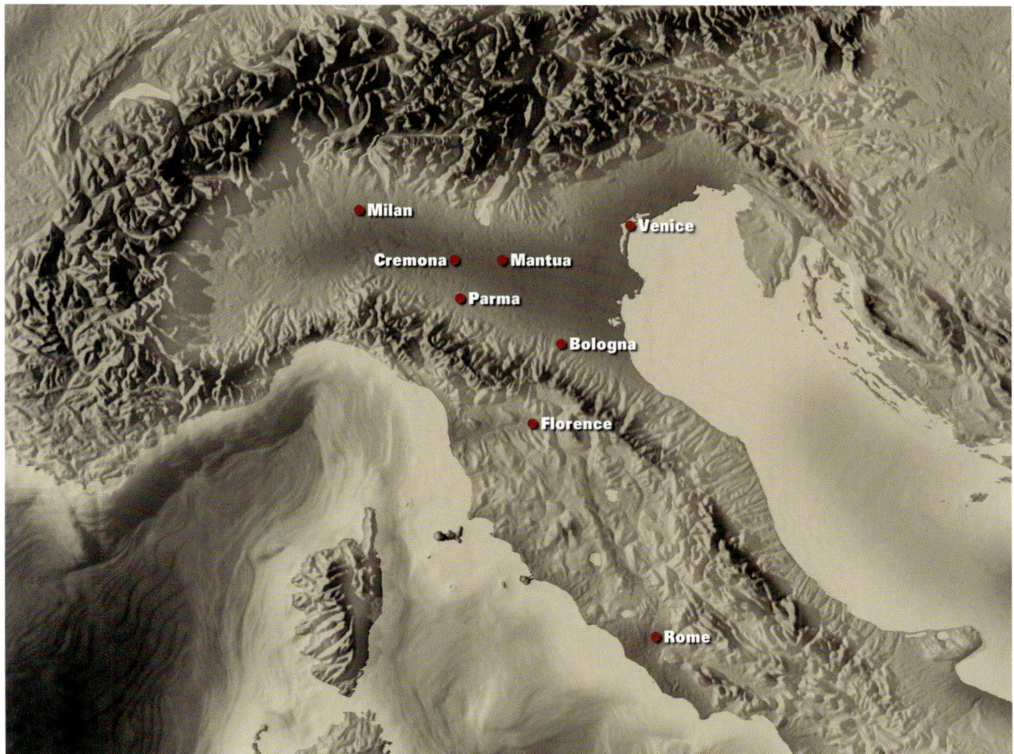

intermediary hands, including those of millers, bakers, and butchers. In the case of veal, the calf would first be sold at the weekly livestock market on the Piazza d'Armi (the present-day Piazza dell'Otto Agosto).[38] The buyer, a butcher, would then take his calf to a place designated for slaughtering, usually in facilities near the Aposa, one of the many canals that traversed Bologna and are now covered up. The final steps in the distribution process would have been the carving and selling of the meat from a market stall like the one depicted in the Kimbell painting. By the time a cut of meat reached the dining table, it had traveled a route that involved herders and livestock sellers as well as the butchers themselves—and I have yet to discuss government regulators and guild officials. Meat was a substantial enterprise that entailed a large workforce—especially during Annibale's earlier life, as the population of Bologna grew toward seventy-five thousand. It was part of an elaborate infrastructure designed to maintain Bologna's main economic engines: cloth, religion, and the university.

Butchers had been operating in Bologna since ancient Roman times, although it was not until the Middle Ages that their fortunes truly began to soar.[39] The watershed moment came during the late twelfth century, when the government of Bologna granted them permission to form their own guild, the Arte dei Beccai.[40] This gave them jurisdiction over their own activities and allowed them to operate as a politically significant bloc. Only two other types of food suppliers received the same concession: the fish vendors and the salt sellers.[41] Neither, however, capitalized on their newly won liberty to the same extent as the butchers. By the 1230s, the butchers' guild was the only one in Bologna to be given license to incorporate itself as its own division of the civil army.[42] It also made several key real-estate investments that allowed it to establish a centralized meat market and slaughterhouse near the commercially important zone of the Porta Ravegnana.[43] The facilities existed in the block of buildings located between the Mercato di Mezzo to the north (the present-day Via Rizzoli), the Via Caprarie to the south, and the Via delle Drapperie to the west (the present-day Via Calzolerie). (See the map of Bologna, figs. 24, 25). That the butchers' guild should select this precise block is not surprising, for butchers had operated in this area for ages—hence the name of the Via Caprarie, which derives from the Italian word for goat, *capra*.[44] Among the several advantages of this block was that water flowed beneath it in the form of the aforementioned Aposa canal. This was critical in that butchers needed a steady

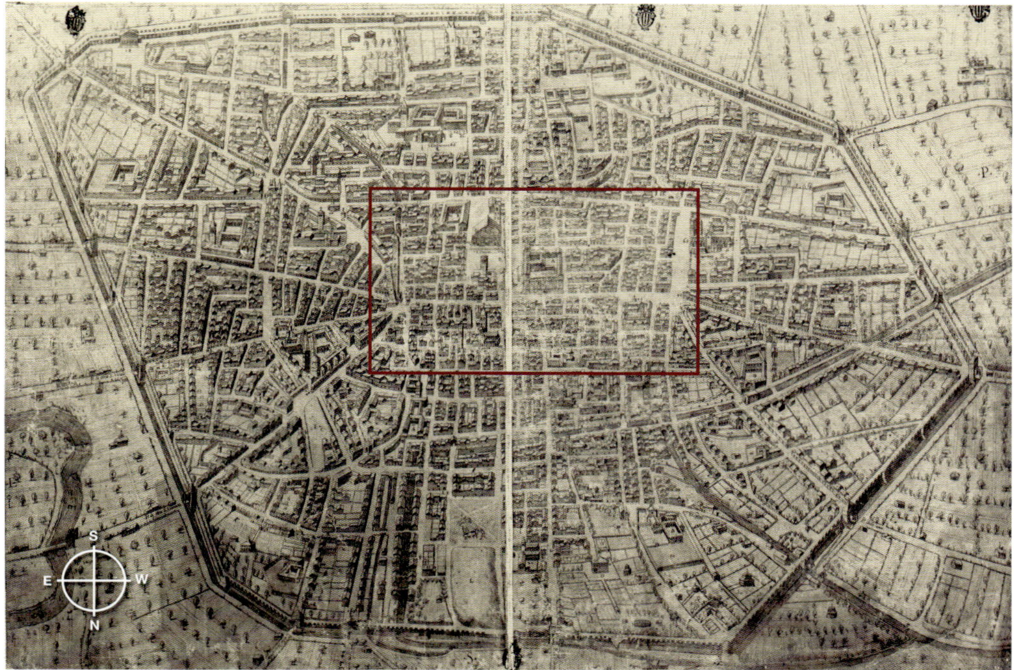

Fig. 24. Agostino Carracci (Italian, 1557–1602) and an unknown artist, *Map of Bologna* (detail), 1581. Engraving, made up of two plates; left: 8¼ x 16⅛ in. (21.1 x 41 cm); right: 8¼ x 16 in. (20.9 x 40.7 cm). Private collection, Bologna

Fig. 25. Agostino Carracci and an unknown artist, *Map of Bologna* (detail of fig. 24). 1.Vaso grande (large butchers' hall); 2. Butchers' guildhall and vaso piccolo (small butchers' hall); 3.Vaso Canobbi; 4.Via Caprarie; 5. Basilica of San Petronio; 6. Santi Gregorio e Siro; 7. Porto Ravegnana; 8. Mercato di Mezzo; 9. Palazzo del Archiginnasio; 10. Palazzo Comunale; 11. Seliciata di San Francesco; 12. Piazza Maggiore

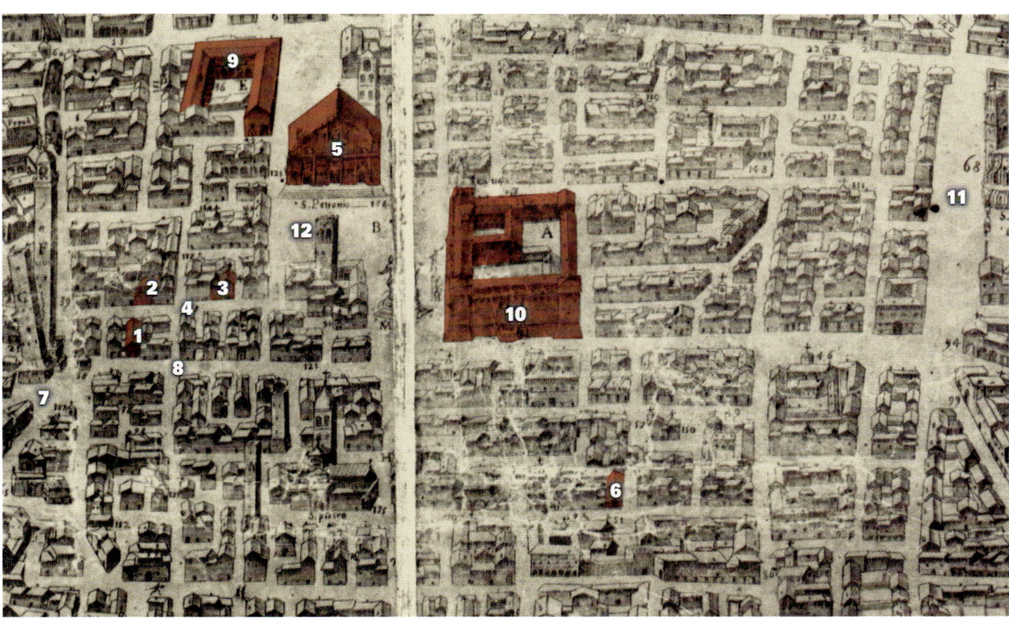

supply of water with which to wash away the blood from slaughter; if it was allowed to pool in the streets, it could be a serious threat to health.

The creation of the complex at the Porta Ravegnana is just one of the many measures that the butchers' guild took during the thirteenth century to ensure its total control over Bologna's butchers. To read the guild statutes from this period is to find long lists of pre-scriptions dealing with who could sell meat, where, and how. By establishing an effective monopoly on the meat supply, the guild sat in a privileged position, and one that it exploited with notable results at various moments between the late twelfth and sixteenth centuries.[45] It eventually rose to a position where members were being regularly tapped for government service, even asked to fill key roles such as that of police chief, or *bargello*.[46] By the dawn of the Renaissance, to belong to the butchers' guild meant a lot more than permission to sell meat. It was a badge of honor, a fact not lost on many of the more politically ambitious men of Bologna, who sometimes joined the butchers' guild for no other reason than to raise their civic profiles. This is one strategy that the famous Bentivoglio family used during the thirteenth and fourteenth centuries to lay the foundation for their eventual hegemony.[47] In 1443, the first of three successive Bentivoglio came to power, ending centuries of republican government.[48] The last and most influential of the usurpers was Giovanni II Bentivoglio, who knew it was politically unwise to make enemies of the butchers. The guild showed its appreciation for his friendship by erecting a tributary inscription to him on the facade of its guildhall in 1490; the inscription is all that survives of the building (fig. 26).[49]

In the fall of 1506, papal troops, led by Pope Julius II himself, arrived in Bologna and put an end to the Bentivoglio's rule. The pope instituted a new senate comprised of forty noblemen of his choosing, and this body was directly accountable to his holiness via an appointed legate.[50] The government was essentially the same when Annibale painted his two butcher's shop pictures during the early 1580s. As already mentioned, the sixteenth century was a time of unprecedented political stability for Bologna, and the economy benefited in numerous ways. For the butchers, economic prosperity brought an expanding population, which translated into increased meat sales. If there was a downside, however, it was that the government took an increasing interest in the butchers and their growing riches and decided that some form of governmental oversight was needed. This was a blow to the butchers'

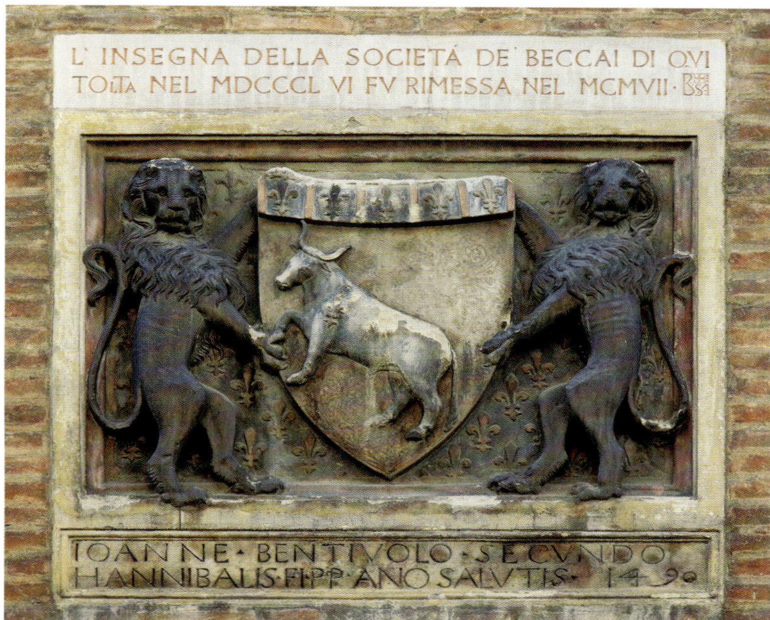

Fig. 26. Tributary inscription dedicated to Giovanni II Bentivoglio, formerly on the facade of the butchers' guildhall, Bologna

guild, which preferred that all matters pertaining to meat be left to its sole discretion. Later in this chapter, we will look at the practical implications of this development, which took a financial toll on the butchers. Fortunately for them, however, their sense of pride remained intact, and there are no signs that their profession suddenly became any less respected in the public eye. Its history was too long and venerable for that.

As far as the public perception of butchers was concerned, the guild delivered a considerable boost only about a decade before the Kimbell *Butcher's Shop* was painted. During the early 1570s, the guild commissioned the city's leading painter, Passarotti, to paint an elaborate altarpiece for its chapel in the basilica of San Petronio (fig. 27).[51] While there were certainly many guilds in Bologna that owned chapels adorned with paintings, what made this commission special was that the butchers' guild was one of only two in Bologna (the other being that of the notaries) granted a chapel in San Petronio, the city's largest and most important church. In spite of popular stereotypes that placed butchers low in the hierarchy of professions, few Bolognese could have ignored the distinction associated with the guild's new altarpiece. Indeed, it served as a timely reminder that being a butcher in Bologna was about a great deal more than the dirty, repetitive work of slaughtering animals,

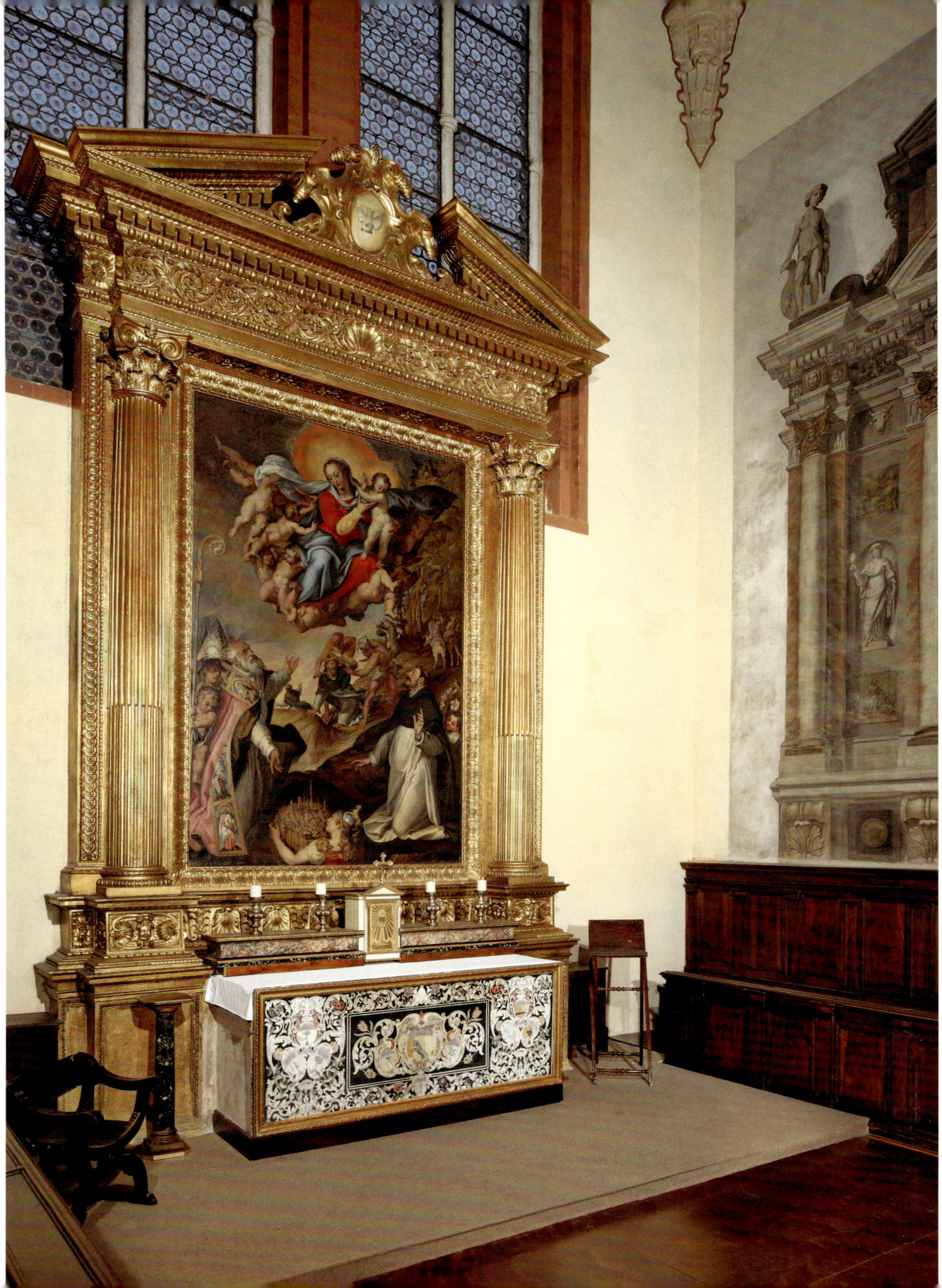

carving them up, and selling their meat. Butchers provided an indispensable civic service, were connected through their guild to prominent businessmen and government officials, and were fairly well-off. These realities—and others to be discussed shortly—must be taken into account when evaluating Annibale's two butcher's shop paintings.

How completely Annibale understood the social position of the butcher can be answered with unusual precision. He was closely related to butchers through his father's side of the family. His uncle, Vincenzo, was a butcher, as was Vincenzo's second son, Giovanni Maria.[52] As for Vincenzo's third son, Ludovico (1555–1619), he would doubtlessly have ended up a butcher had he not discovered a love for painting and become a painter like his cousin Annibale. At the age of five, Ludovico was enrolled in the butchers' guild, and we can safely wager that many of his childhood days were spent helping his father at his stall.[53] Indeed, Ludovico was probably well on his way to becoming a full-fledged butcher's apprentice when—perhaps around the age of twelve or thirteen—he pledged himself to painting, joining the studio of Prospero Fontana.[54] This may have factored into Fontana's decision to nickname his new pupil "the ox," or "*il bue.*"[55] Ludovico was reportedly a slow learner, and Fontana likely intended the nickname as a swipe at his simple background.[56] Ludovico broke quickly with Fontana and was soon off teaching himself, traveling first to Florence and then to the principal cities of northern Italy, including Parma and Venice. It was only a matter of time before he had embarked on one of the most impressive careers in the history of Bolognese painting, a career that owed much to Annibale. Despite Ludovico's being five years older than his cousin, the two painters grew to be exceptionally close and were already sharing a studio by the early 1580s.[57] It seems inconceivable that Annibale could have spent so much time with Ludovico and not gained an insider's perspective into how Ludovico's family earned their living. There must also have been plenty of occasions when Annibale was in the presence of his uncle and the talk turned to matters of his profession.

One question that may have arisen during such discussions is why Vincenzo chose to be a butcher rather than to follow his two brothers and become a tailor. Both Annibale's father, Antonio, and his other uncle, Carlo, were third-generation tailors.[58] We might

Fig. 27. The Chapel of the Butchers' Guild, Basilica of San Petronio, Bologna, with Bartolomeo Passarotti's *Martyrdom of Saint Peter Martyr with the Virgin in Glory with Saints Petronius and Dominic* (c. 1570–75)

understand Vincenzo's choice better if being a butcher were superior in terms of money or social standing.[59] But it was not. Butchers typically earned less than tailors, and their work was dirtier and not thought to require the same intelligence.[60] The distinction may have been particularly sharp in the case of Vincenzo and Antonio. Antonio had a flourishing career in Bologna, serving many in the highest ranks of the nobility, such as Filippo Fava, an important early patron of the three Carracci painters, which included Annibale's older brother, the gifted painter and printmaker Agostino (1557–1602).[61] Social status was important to Antonio, and he appears to have strategized at length about how to improve his sons' places in society—hence, his decision to enroll them in grammar school, a luxury that does not seem to have been afforded to Ludovico.[62]

Much to Annibale's credit, however, any differences in social class that may have existed between him and his cousin never appear to have been a factor in their relationship. Annibale was that rare person who, even if smart, worldly, and a constant champion of the nobility of his profession, maintained a down-to-earth attitude toward his fellow human beings.[63] As many of his drawings attest—including, it seems, the astonishing *Hunchback Boy* at Chatsworth House (fig. 28)—he enjoyed going into the streets of Bologna and turning his sympathetic eye toward the city's less fortunate, who he drew with unusual compassion.[64] Even in Rome, when surrounded by princes and cardinals and at the height of his career, Annibale remained most comfortable in the presence of common folk. The one time he was reportedly insulted for belonging to "the race of butchers" (la razza di macellari), it is unlikely that he really cared.[65] He was brought up among people who earned their living with their hands, and it was never his nature to take on airs to impress a social superior.[66] Nor was he the sort who took pleasure in making people of a lower rank feel inferior. This all suggests that in his dealings with his uncle, he would have been entirely admiring and deferential and thought nothing shameful about his uncle's chosen line of work. It may even be the case that Vincenzo encouraged these feelings by reminding his nephew about the storied history of the butchers' guild and how the profession—at least in Bologna—carried considerable honor.[67]

The main way to substantiate Annibale's sympathies for butchers is to appreciate his sensitive treatment of them in his two butcher's shop paintings. In both, he breaks

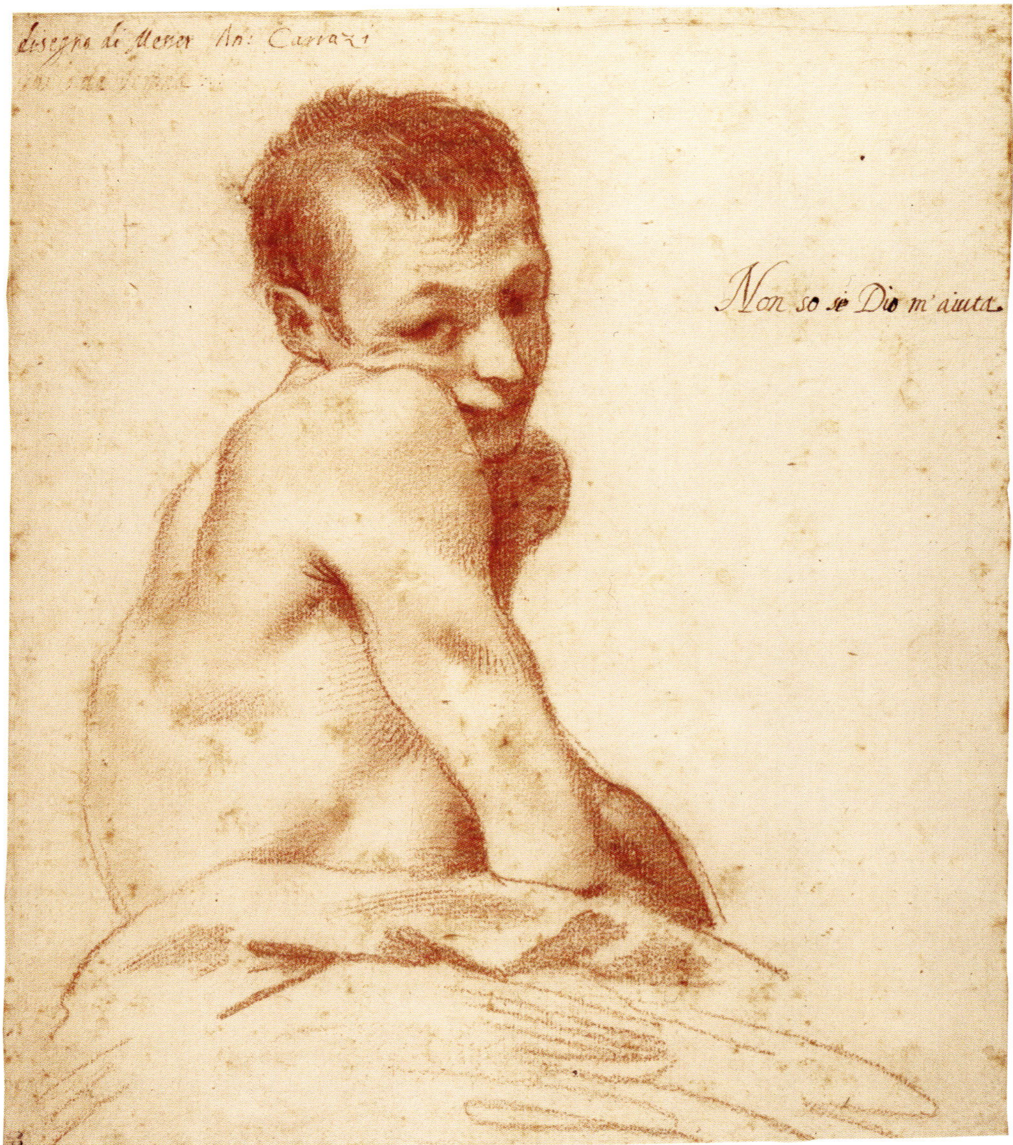

Fig. 28. Annibale Carracci (Italian, 1560–1609), *Hunchback Boy*, mid-1580s. Red chalk, 10⅜ x 8⅞ in. (26.4 x 22.5 cm). Duke of Devonshire and the Chatsworth Settlement Trustees

with tradition and casts his butchers as honest, hardworking individuals—not as comic characters. This difference has given rise to suggestions that the Oxford *Butcher's Shop* is a group portrait of the Carracci family in the guise of butchers.[68] While the faces do give a strong impression of portraiture, there are good reasons for this theory to be dismissed.[69]

First, there is no agreement on which butcher represents which Carracci, as we do not really know how Annibale, Ludovico, or Agostino looked at this time.[70] Secondly, unless Vincenzo was a very young father, none of the butchers seem quite old enough to be him.[71] The third and most convincing argument is that the size and attendant cost of the painting make it exceedingly unlikely that any member of the Carracci family could have been the patron. Moreover, why would some other family have wanted a portrait of the Carracci? The painting went to someone with deep pockets and who had a large enough room in which to display it. Another consideration is that, given the painting's sympathetic outlook toward butchers, the patron is likely to have been someone who depended on butchers for his or her well-being. This is not to rule out that we may still be looking at actual butchers—perhaps even ones Annibale knew. But the chances seem to diminish once we begin to dig deeper into the painting's meaning. In all probability, these are simply studio models that Annibale *posed* as butchers.

Addressing this issue, it is first important to consider the type of person who might have commissioned the painting. As already discussed, membership in the butchers' guild was not limited to common butchers. Anyone with a financial stake in the meat trade typically belonged, and since meat could be highly lucrative, this group was usually sizeable. One of the most common investing strategies was to buy up the rights to butcher's stalls and to lease them to individual butchers. The system worked because the guild regulated how many stalls could operate in the city.[72] Through the acquisition of the rights to stalls, it was possible to form a sort of commercial empire founded on the sale of meat. During the 1560s, two members of the wealthy Canobbi family, Giuseppe and Girolamo, took this business model to new heights, and it has been speculated that one of them must have been the original owner of the Oxford *Butcher's Shop*.[73] In 1564, the Canobbi agreed to build a new butcher's complex (a large building housing multiple stalls) at their own expense near the existing one at the Porta Ravegnana.[74] (The precise location was on the Via degli Orefici in the block of buildings faced on the west by the Via delle Drapperie and on the south by the Via delle Pescherie Vecchie; see the map of Bologna, figs. 24, 25.) In exchange for covering the building costs, the Canobbi received rights to all the butcher's stalls that went into the new complex, a not inconsiderable number.[75] The 1560s saw a major push on the part of the government to move the city's butcher's stalls off the streets and into three complexes, or butchers' halls, near the Porta Ravegnana.[76] The oldest and largest of these, which had been in use since the middle of the thirteenth century and was called the *vaso grande* (the large hall or space), was located between the Mercato di Mezzo (the present-day Via Rizzoli) and the Via Caprarie. The second was smaller—hence its name, the *vaso piccolo*—and occupied the ground floor of the butchers' guildhall on the south side of the Via Caprarie. The newest was the Canobbi's. In total, thirty stalls operated within the complexes, and there were another four stalls that were sanctioned to operate in the distant neighborhoods of the city.[77] What these numbers suggest is that the Canobbi effectively controlled between a quarter and a third of all meat sales in Bologna. Needless to say, they sat on a moneymaker, and the resulting wealth helped them to gain all the trappings of a properly aristocratic family— including a private chapel in a prominent church, Santi Gregorio e Siro, complete with an altarpiece by a respectable artist. In this case, the artist selected proved to be Annibale, and the altarpiece in question was his masterful *Baptism of Christ*, finished in 1585 (fig. 29).[78] It is hard not to imagine that he won the commission because he had already supplied the Canobbi with the Oxford *Butcher's Shop*.

While we may never know for certain whether or not a member of the Canobbi family commissioned the Oxford *Butcher's Shop*, the painting's true message seems custom-made for the Canobbi—or, if not for them, for a very similar family. Indeed, the painting combines a number of details into a statement about the difficulties of trying to reap a profit from a butcher's stall during the early 1580s in Bologna. The problem did not reside with the butchers, who are portrayed as honest and hardworking. It was the government that was to blame, and the conflict centered on price controls.[79] As Bologna's population expanded during the sixteenth century, the supply of meat had a difficult time keeping pace, and the government began to institute price controls to keep meat affordable. The butchers (and families like the Canobbi) were angry because their costs had gone up—especially as more and more meat had to be imported. The government maintained a hard line and became wise to the possibility that some butchers might try to cheat the system by adjusting their scales to yield favorable prices, a practice called short-weighing. In an effort to curb this fraudulent activity, the government created what amounted to a butcher's police. Agents

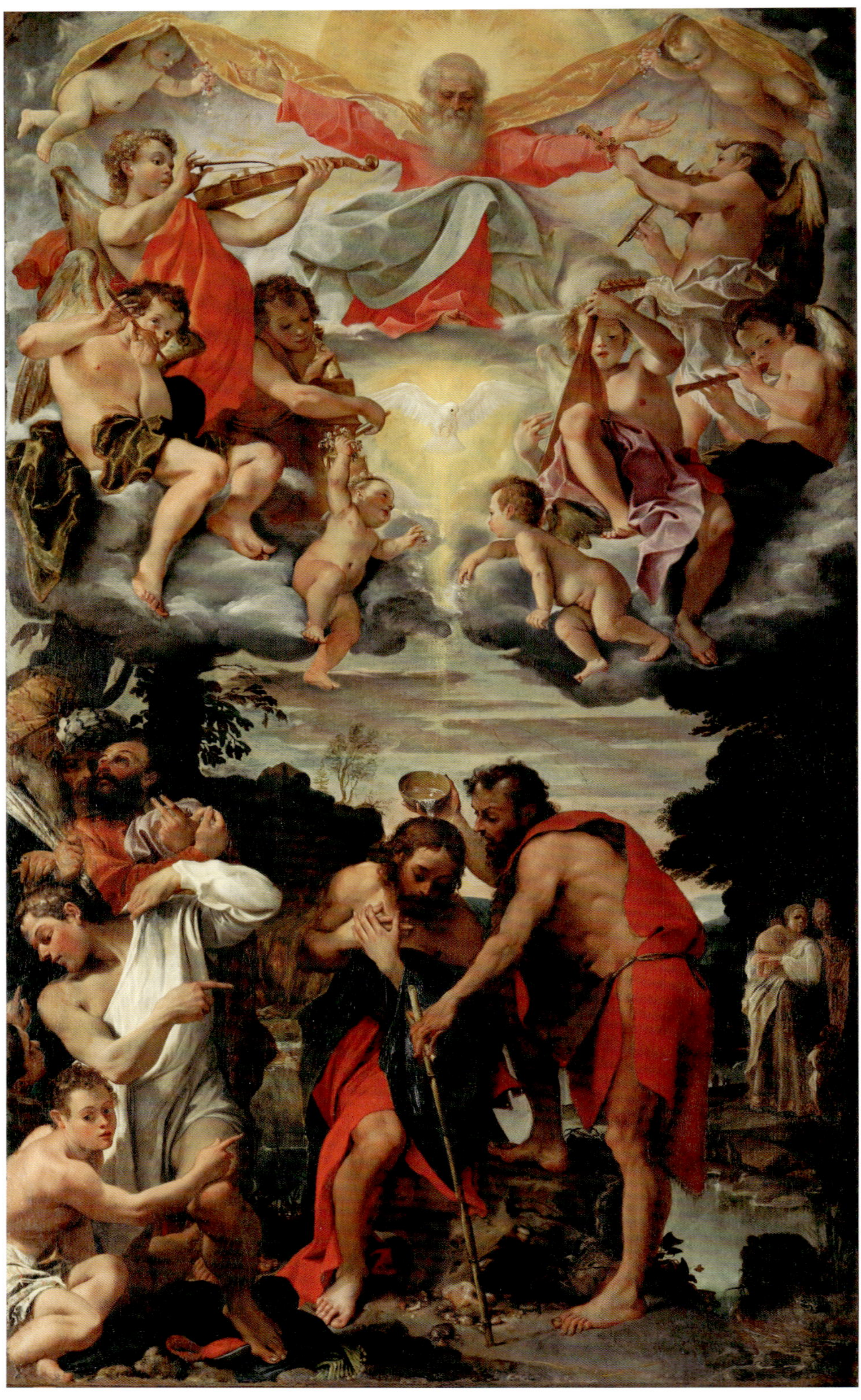

Opposite page:
Fig. 29. Annibale Carracci (Italian, 1560–1609),
The Baptism of Christ, 1585. Oil on canvas,
150¾ x 88⅝ in. (383 x 225 cm). Church of Santi
Gregorio e Siro, Bologna

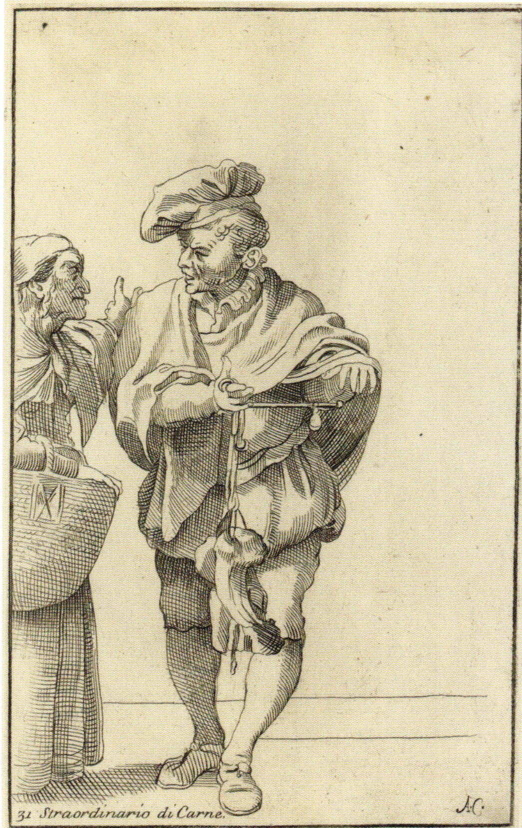

Fig. 30. Simon Guillain II (French, born 1618,
active 1646), *Straordinario di carne*, engraving from
Le Arti di Bologna, Rome, 1646, pl. 31, after a drawing
by Annibale Carracci from the late 1580s or early 1590s.
Print Collection, Miriam and Ira D. Wallach Division
of Art, Prints and Photographs, The New York Public
Library, Astor, Lenox and Tilden Foundations

would patrol the city and, on spotting an individual with a fresh cut of meat, verify that
he or she had paid the correct price. In the event of a discrepancy, a fine would be levied
against the offending butcher. These patrolmen, called *straordinari di carne*, became familiar
sights on the streets of Bologna, and Annibale illustrated one in his *Arti di Bologna*, or *Trades
of Bologna*, a series of seventy-five drawings of common tradesmen and market workers that
he made during the late 1580s or early 1590s.[80] All but one of the drawings are now lost, but
the series was fortunately engraved and published in 1646.[81] In the print labeled *Straordinario
di carne*, we see the government agent weighing a cut of meat presumably just purchased by
the woman on the left (fig. 30). The woman bears a strong resemblance to the crone in the
background of the Oxford *Butcher's Shop*. She plays the role of the stock customer—in this
case, one who might actually cooperate with the straordinario di carne to catch a butcher
at cheating.

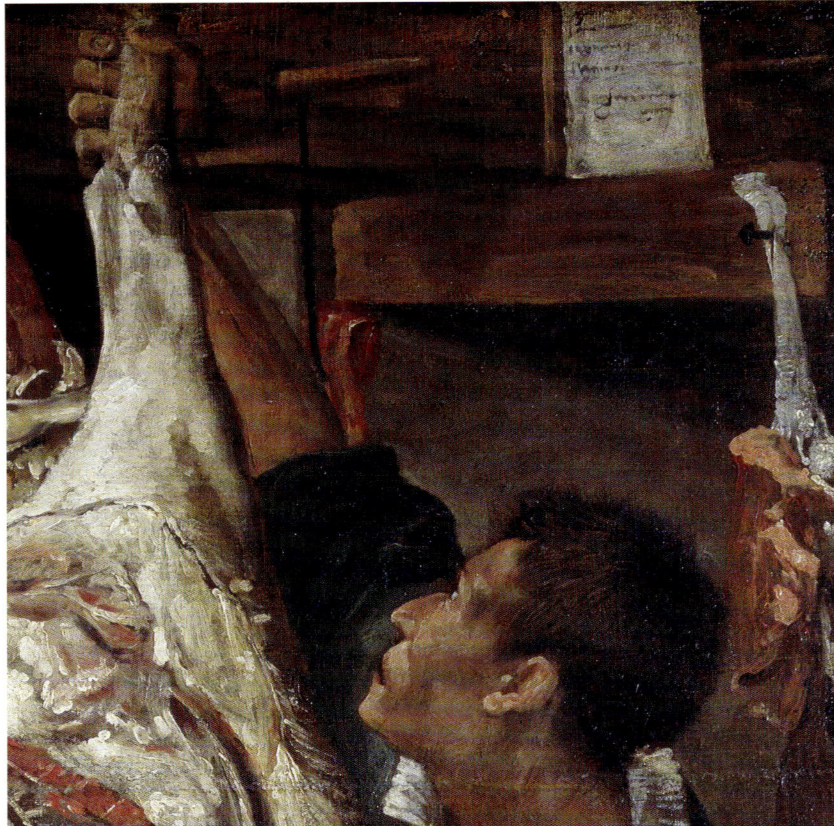

There are four other ways in which the Oxford *Butcher's Shop* acknowledges the issue of price controls. The first is the piece of paper with writing tacked to the nearest rafter, which is doubtless the official price-control list that all butchers were required to display in their stalls (fig. 31).[82] The second is the prominence that Annibale gives the act of weighing in his composition and the fact that the butcher who does the weighing shows no signs of deviousness. The third is the almost equal conspicuousness of the butcher at the back who reaches overhead for a branch of willow (fig. 32).[83] Unlike today, meat was not wrapped in paper after purchasing. It was tied with a length of strong vine to form a sort of handle for carrying. The practice was largely maintained for the sake of the *straordinari di carne*, who did not want people to be able to sneak their meat home unseen. Finally, there is the Swiss guard on the left, who can be interpreted as a symbol of the Bolognese government. It has

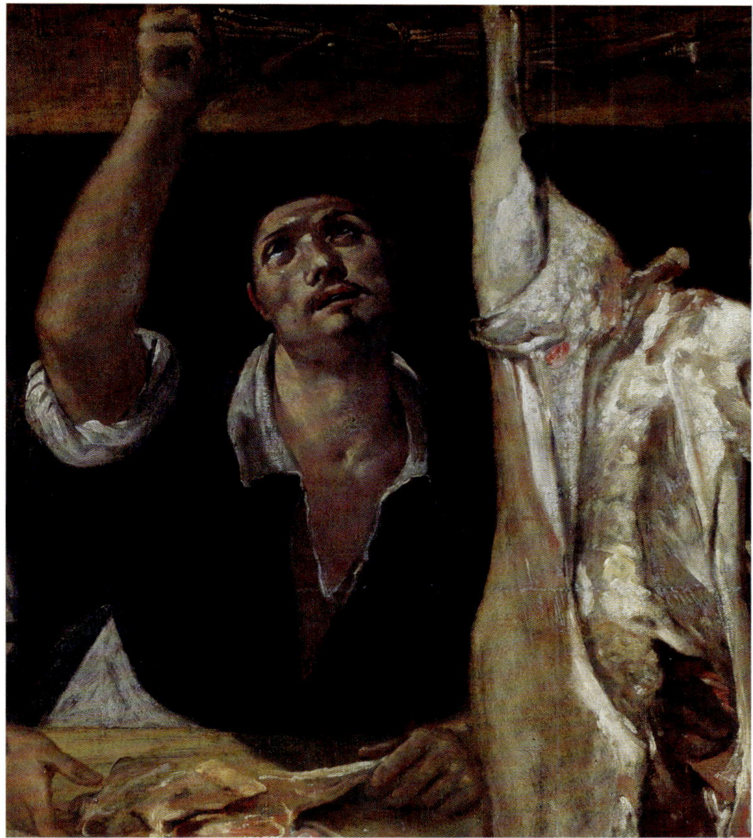

Fig. 32. Annibale Carracci, Oxford *Butcher's Shop*, detail (see fig. 6)

been rightly observed that no Swiss guard would ever buy meat from an ordinary butcher's stall, as the pope's men were exempt from taxes and regulations and could slaughter their own livestock.[84] His presence in the painting must therefore be symbolic. He stands for the pope's government, and his distinctive costume ensured that no contemporary could mistake him as anything else. Thus, his clumsy pose, which borders on laughable, becomes more readily explained. It suggests the contempt that butchers and families such as the Canobbi felt toward the government.[85] We also see more clearly now why Annibale may have chosen to base his composition on Michelangelo's and Raphael's frescoes of *The Sacrifice of Noah*. Any astute viewer with pro-butcher leanings would have appreciated the idea that an average butcher could assume the role of a sacred character in a major work of "high" art. Moreover, a socially ambitious family such as the Canobbi is likely to have taken a certain comfort in

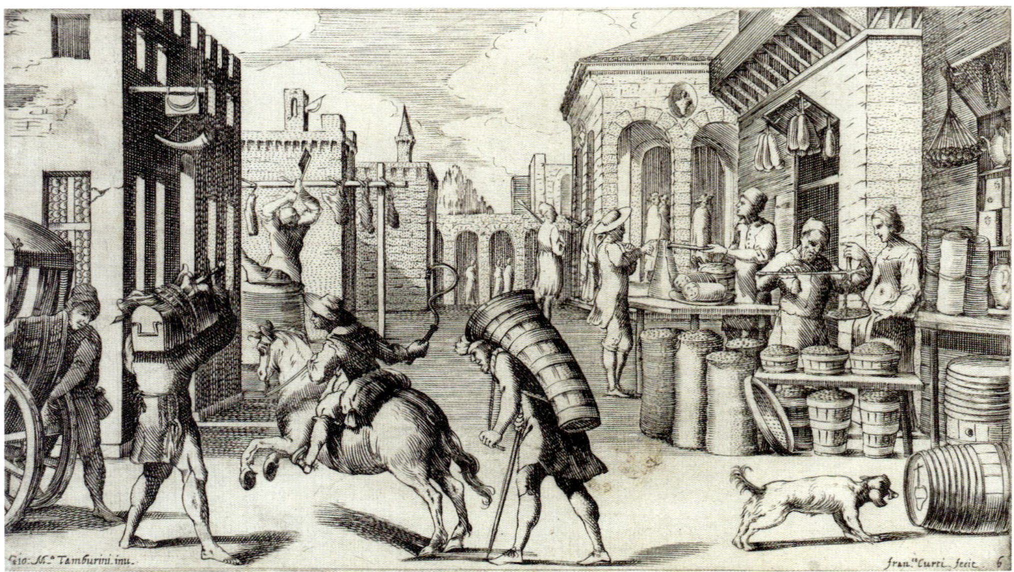

Fig. 33. Francesco Curti (Italian, 1603–1670), *Trades of Bologna*, c. 1640, after a drawing by Giovanni Maria Tamburini (Italian, died after 1660). Etching, sheet: 7¾ x 11⁷⁄₁₆ in. (19.7 x 29.1 cm); image: 5⅛ x 9⁹⁄₁₆ in. (13 x 23 cm). Los Angeles County Museum of Art. Graphic Arts Council Curatorial Discretionary Fund, M.69.7.1f

thinking about their business interests in these elevated terms. This serves as a further indication that the Oxford *Butcher's Shop* is not a transcription of butchers at work. It is a carefully staged painting meant to deliver a message for a patron with an agenda. It is easy to imagine the huge canvas hanging in a prominent room in a palazzo—whether the Canobbi's or some other such family's—where it served to remind its owners of how they became wealthy and the challenges they faced in remaining so.

When we shift to the Kimbell *Butcher's Shop*, the political overtones disappear, and we seem to be looking at what the Oxford *Butcher's Shop* is so emphatically not: a plein-air record of butchers going about their business on a typical day. But are we? From the standpoint of factual accuracy, the answer appears to be yes. A good starting point is the structure and its physical surroundings. There is no reason to think that Annibale has invented these parts wholesale, although confirmation is not totally straightforward. The main obstacle is that there are no good illustrations of butcher's stalls from the period apart from Annibale's two paintings. Nor is there one that can be reliably identified among the many topographic views of Bologna that survive from the eighteenth and nineteenth centuries. The single useful point of comparison is a print from around 1650 that is based on a drawing by the Bolognese painter and draftsman Giovanni Maria Tamburini (fig. 33).[86] In the background is a butcher chopping meat with a cleaver. His stall appears to be freestanding, to be set in a small piazza, and to consist of no more than a single rafter hung with four pieces of meat. There are obvious analogies with the stall depicted in the Kimbell *Butcher's Shop*—the wooden rafter, the round chopping block—although caution must be exercised in placing too much stock in the print's documentary value. It comes from a series representing the trades of Bologna, and the artist has clearly been schematic in his approach in order to fit as many trades as possible into his scene. All we can reasonably conclude is that in seventeenth-century Bologna wooden rafters and round chopping blocks were commonly associated with butcher's stalls.

However limited the print may be in confirming how the typical Bolognese butcher's stall looked around 1580, it does draw attention to a key issue, that of the "outdoor" stall (located on a street) versus the "indoor" stall (located in one of the butchers' halls). In the print, the butcher sells his meat outdoors, which cannot be assumed to be the case in the Kimbell *Butcher's Shop*. As noted above, Annibale's painting dates from a time when only about ten percent of Bologna's butcher's stalls were located outdoors. The remainder were under cover in the three complexes near the Porta Ravegnana. It seems likely, therefore, that in selecting a model for the Kimbell *Butcher's Shop*, Annibale would have chosen from among the more prevalent indoor type. The risk with this assumption, however, is that Annibale may have been much more familiar with the outdoor type owing to the fact that his uncle is documented in 1587 as being the proprietor of the outdoor stall located at the Seliciata di San Francesco (present-day Piazza Malpighi; see fig. 25).[87] This was one of four stalls sanctioned to operate in the outlying neighborhoods of Bologna. Frustratingly, we do not know when Vincenzo took up this location, as he could well have been working in one of the complexes throughout the time Annibale was concerned with his butcher's shop paintings. More critically, there are sufficient clues in the painting that it seems almost certain that Annibale has based his stall on the kind he knew from the complexes—not from the streets.

Concerning this argument, the first challenge is to imagine what the interiors of the complexes looked like. None survive, and we only have views of the exteriors. During the 1910s and early 1920s, the Via Caprarie was enlarged, and the vaso grande, which was located on the north side of the street, was demolished, giving way to the street as it appears today (fig. 34).[88] Meanwhile, the two complexes on the south side of the street—the vaso piccolo (located in the butchers' guildhall) and the vaso Canobbi—were also razed. Fortunately, in the case of the vaso grande, there is a photograph from the early twentieth century showing how its entrance on the Via Caprarie then looked (fig. 36).[89] While the facade probably reflects refurbishments from when the building was converted into a fish market in the eighteenth century, the photograph provides an important clue about the interior: it was narrow.[90] This description can be expanded to *long* and narrow by taking account of the famous map of Bologna of 1581, often attributed to Agostino, that shows the vaso grande as extending from the Via Caprarie all the way across to the old Mercato del Mezzo, a distance of approximately fifty meters (fig. 35).[91] The interior thus resembled a long hall

Fig. 34. View of the Via Caprarie from the Piazza della Mercanzia, Bologna

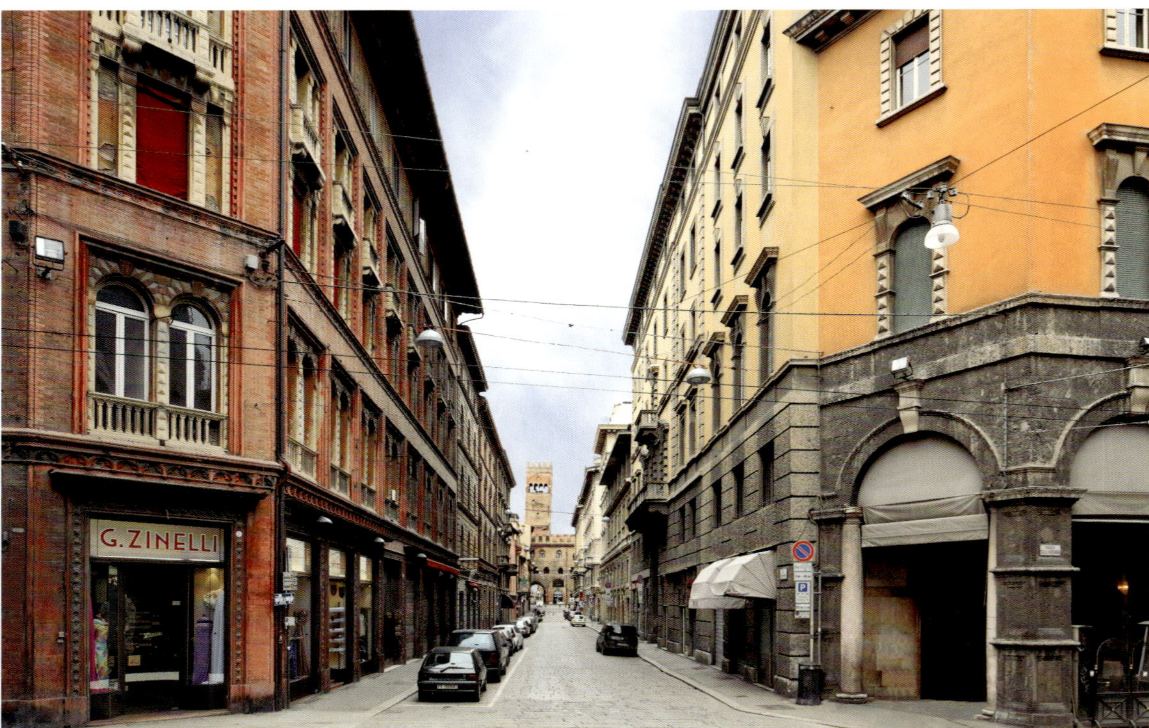

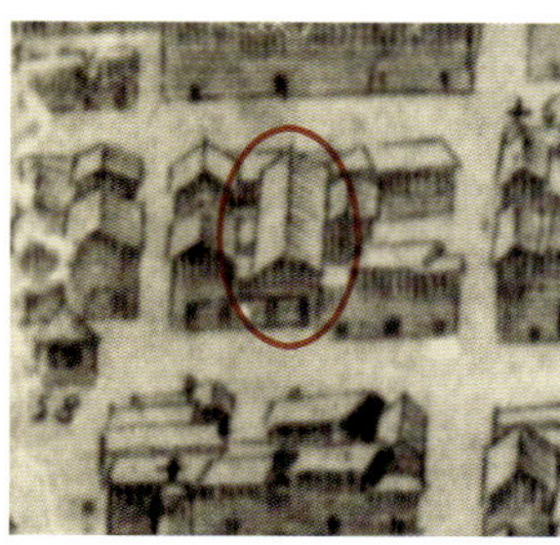

Fig. 35. Agostino Carracci
and an unknown artist, *Map of
Bologna*, detail of the *vaso grande*
(large butchers' hall) (see fig. 25)

with entrances on both ends. The stalls would have been placed against the walls in two rows facing each other, and we can assume that the aisle between them was tight. (Imagine Annibale trying to erect an easel in this space and paint without being constantly jostled.) As for the ceiling, Agostino's map suggests that it was pitched, which indicates basic timber construction, perhaps covered in terracotta tiles.[92]

Fig. 36. Arnaldo Romagnoli (Italian, 1875–1930), view of the north side of the Via Caprarie from the Piazza della Mercanzia, indicating the south entrance of the vaso grande, Bologna, 1912–16, photograph. Collezioni d'Arte e di Storia della Fondazione Cassa di Risparmio in Bologna

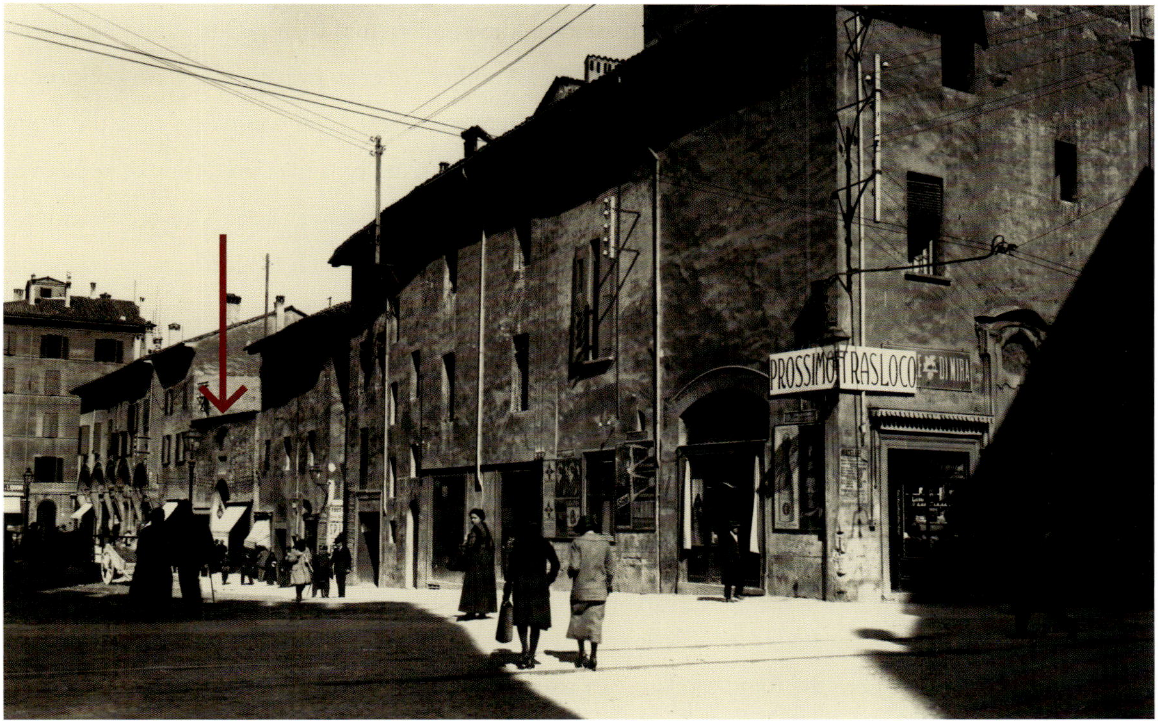

Similar obstacles present themselves in reconstructing the vaso piccolo and the vaso Canobbi. The vaso piccolo was located on the ground floor of the butchers' guildhall, which had stood since the fourteenth century.[93] The upper story was where the guild met and transacted its business, and it seems to have featured a high, pitched ceiling—possibly even vaulted. Beneath the meeting room was a more utilitarian space given over to the preparation and selling of meat. This space appears to have resembled the vaso grande in being long and narrow and was probably organized in two rows of facing stalls with an aisle for customers between them.[94] The vaso Canobbi seems to have shared this layout. According to the available evidence, it was a virtual duplicate of the vaso grande, just somewhat shorter.[95] While many more questions of appearance remain—what was the composition of the ceiling? were there any rooms?—we are at least fortunate to know that each butcher's complex was seemingly designed with the idea that its interior walls should be lined with stalls such as the one depicted in the Kimbell *Butcher's Shop*.

A different direction from which to approach the question of "indoor" versus "outdoor" is to consider how well suited the stall in the painting seems for a street-front location.[96] Its open architecture is less than ideal; the butchers and their goods would have been unduly exposed to the elements and traffic. Another concern is that there is no back room where the butchers might store their equipment overnight. The complexes near the Porta Ravegnana solved these problems. There was cover, security, a measured flow of pedestrian traffic, and ample space for dedicated storage rooms, possibly shared. The only elements in the painting that suggest the outdoors are the shadows, which fall left to right and seem unusually strong for an indoor setting in a preelectrical age. Moreover, a warm and even light bathes the butchers, which might also seem incompatible with the indoors. What must be taken into account, however, is that most commercial spaces in Renaissance Bologna were designed with large windows and skylights, and these could easily have permitted the kind of lighting effects that appear in the painting.[97]

If doubts remain about the indoor setting, the head of the sheep in the foreground and the dead lamb just to the left of the table should quell them. These are evidence of fresh slaughter, which was unwelcome (if not outright prohibited) in the residential areas of Bologna, where the four "satellite," or street-front, stalls were located. Since the thirteenth century, the guild had worked hard to restrict the bloodiest parts of butchering—killing and gutting—to its facilities near the Porta Ravegnana, and the government lent its weight to the initiative during the 1560s with the construction of the three butchers' halls fronting the Via Caprarie.[98] Although documentation for the 1580s is scarce, there is almost certain to have been some type of government or guild prohibition against the slaughter and gutting of livestock on the open streets—anywhere but the butchers' halls.[99] The reasons are obvious: killing animals was unsightly, smelly, and potentially loud, and there were also serious sanitation concerns.

That the stall pictured in the Kimbell *Butcher's Shop* seems likely to be of the prevailing indoor type offers additional evidence that Annibale intended his scene to be interpreted as real, not imagined. The painting is accurate in other important ways. The two suspended carcasses incorporate a great deal of anatomic specificity, enabling us to be reasonably certain about which kinds of meat are being sold. The carcass on the left is a calf, while the one on the right is probably a lamb (fig. 37).[100] These—in addition to the sheep's head in the foreground and the dead lamb or goat near the left leg of the table—indicate that Annibale has represented a specific kind of butcher's stall. It is a *beccaria di minuto*, which was restricted to selling the meat of small livestock: mutton, goat, lamb, and veal.[101] There were other butchers who handled beef and pork, and the separation was strictly enforced by the guild. Another detail involves the white aprons worn by the two butchers. To modern eyes, they may look implausibly clean. But the truth is that in Renaissance Italy, there was a strong association between cleanliness and white linens.[102] Given all the energy expended in Bologna on maintaining a sanitized environment for the sale of meat, and given the constant push on the part of the butchers to make themselves respected in Bolognese society, it would make sense that they kept extra aprons on hand into which they changed before dealing with customers. Admittedly, the practice is not documented, and we may be witness to a ploy by Annibale to improve the image of his butchers. But hygiene seems to have been enough of a concern in butchers' circles that some premium must have been placed on how they presented themselves publicly, and crisp, white aprons would have been an easy and obvious way for them to look clean.[103]

So far, this chapter has focused on the many ways that the Kimbell *Butcher's Shop* reflects

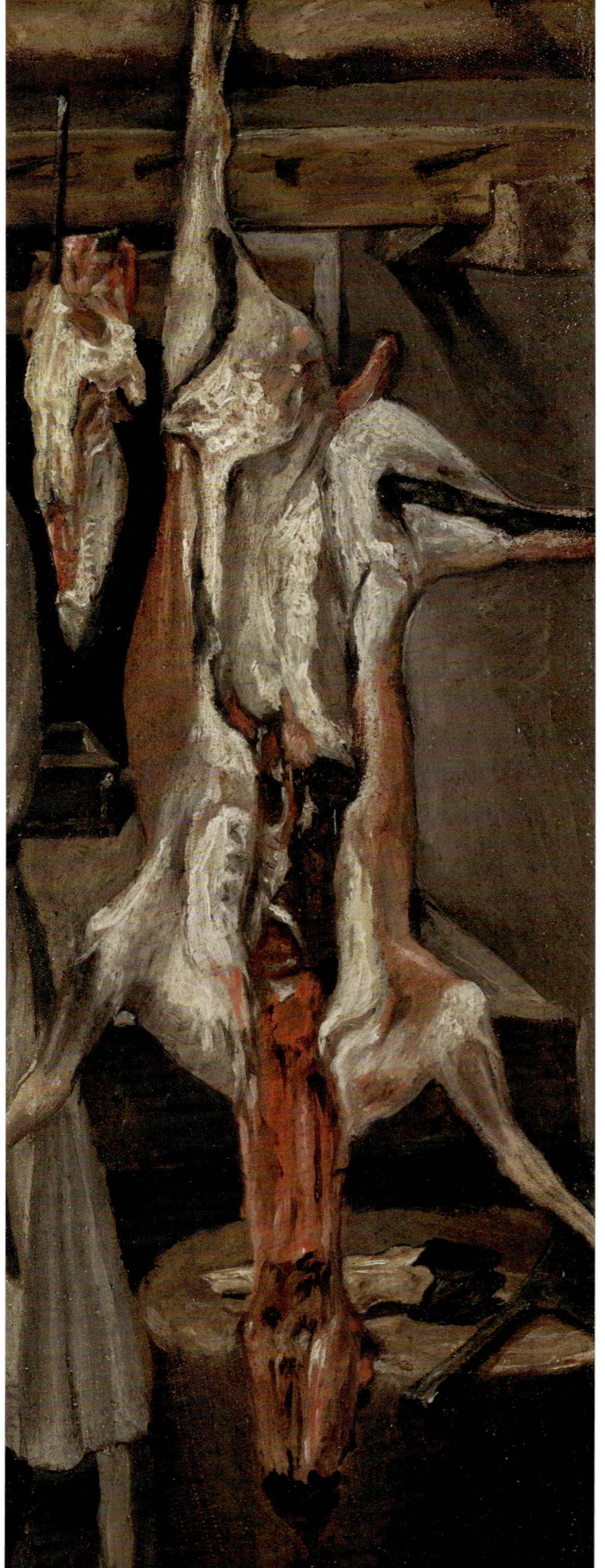

50 **Fig. 37**. Annibale Carracci, Kimbell
Butcher's Shop, detail (see fig. 1)

reality. In at least a few ways, however, it does not. One omission is the list of price controls that was supposed to be visible in all butcher's stalls in Bologna. The white piece of paper (or cloth) hanging from the rafter in the distant background is unlikely to be this list, as it is too large and shows no writing. Another element that seems to have been ignored is the composition of the floor. It is depicted as smooth and tan with no noticeable pattern of cobbling or paving. The temptation is to interpret it as earthen, but it is far more likely that the butcher's complexes were floored in durable bricks, which would have allowed for easy washing. Annibale may simply have felt that to render each brick was too painstaking and that all the finicky lines would have distracted from other parts of the painting. Either way, the discrepancy with the floor—as with the absence of the price-control list—neither confirms nor denies that Annibale painted the Kimbell *Butcher's Shop* in front of an actual butcher's stall. It only suggests that his approach to naturalism was not rooted in details. His goal was to convey the experience of direct observation, and he knew that he could miss a detail or two without compromising the illusion.

Where the illusion is threatened, however, is with the large wooden table in the background. The longer we look at it, the more we realize that Annibale must have imagined its appearance back in his studio. One issue is the tilt. It looks to be gently tilted up toward us, which suggests that its function was that of a display table. This is perfectly appropriate in the context of a market stall, although we must wonder why the forward edges of the table (left and right) are not slightly canted inwards in accordance with the rules of perspective, assuming the table is solid. Other parts of the table might also give us pause. Only two legs are visible, and it is strange that they are not set at the front corners but well toward the center and at a good distance back from the front edge. This placement would seem to jeopardize the table's stability. Perhaps the table's entire back edge is intended to be attached to the wall, which would explain why there are no back legs and why the recess is so shallow.

However long we stare at the table, the impression that Annibale could have made it a great deal more legible does not diminish. Our instinct is to assume that the curious table began as flat and was consciously manipulated so that the meat on it became more visible. Interestingly, this is how the filmmaker Philip Haas recently interpreted the creation of the

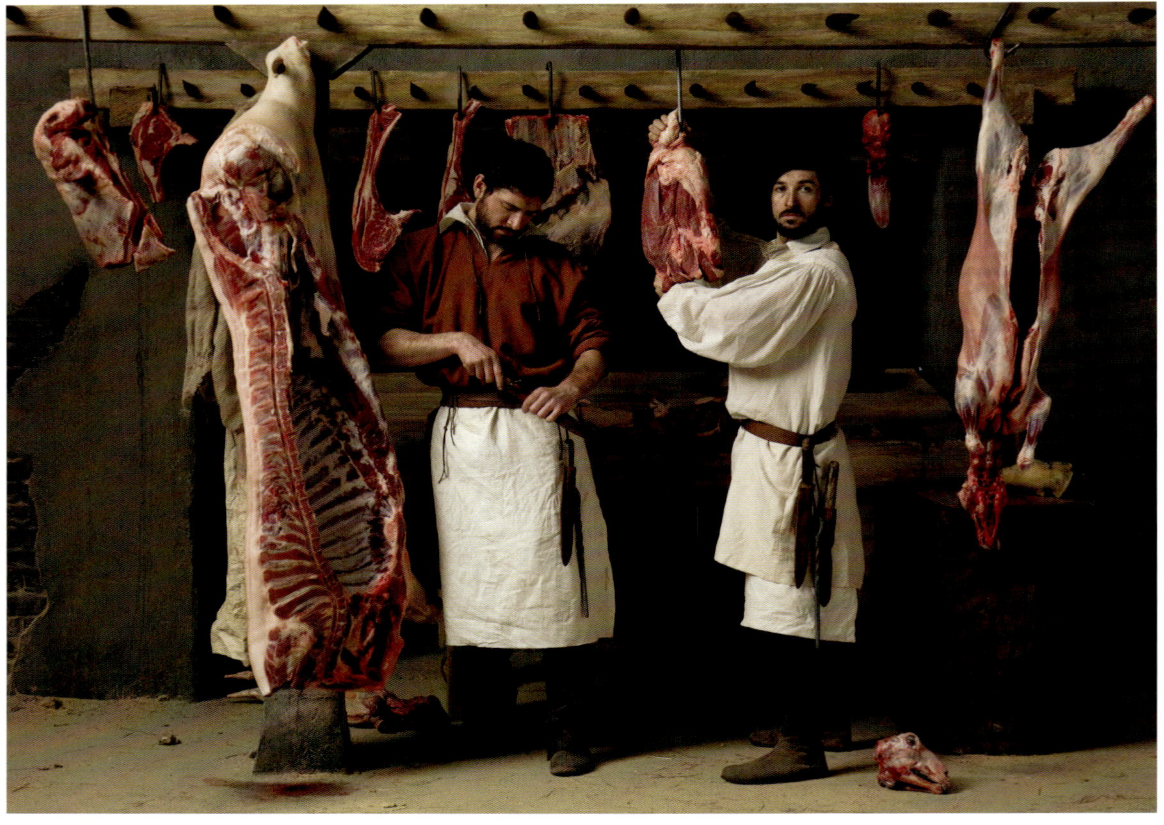

Fig. 38. Philip Haas (American, born 1954), film still from "The Butcher's Shop": re-creation of the Kimbell painting by Annibale Carracci, 2009

painting (fig. 38).[104] He recognized that in order to re-create the scene (fig. 39), the table must be tilted, and he actually included a moment in his film when the two butchers raise the back of the table on blocks so that Annibale can see the meat on it. This maneuver did not fix everything, however, and Haas was forced to admit that unless he suspended his normal assumptions about the shape of certain objects, the painting could not be re-created perfectly. Consider the difficulties he faced in reproducing the left edge of the tabletop, which, from a perspectival point of view, Annibale has not oriented vertically enough. The artist appears to have improvised the perspective rather than to have worked it out rigorously, based on a combination of direct observation and mathematics. While the Kimbell *Butcher's Shop* may be consistent with virtually all we know about real butcher's stalls in early-1580s Bologna, it is by no means the perfect picture of reality in every way. It is like any painting. Its imagery has passed through its creator's mind, not always leaving as it entered.

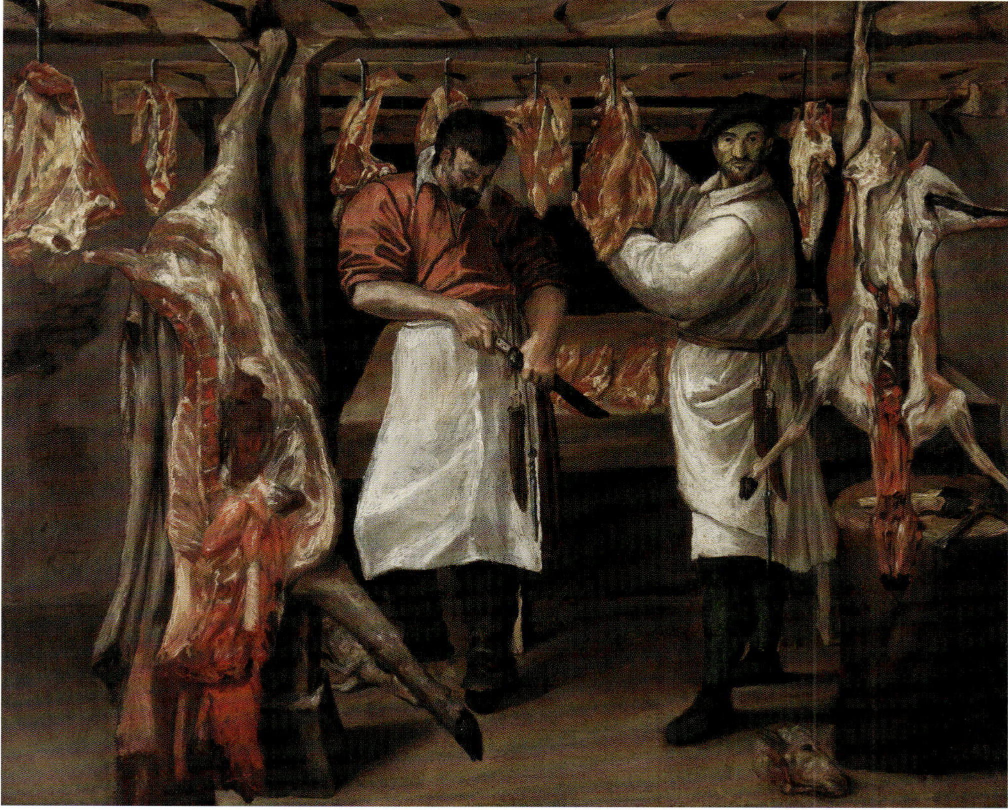

Fig. 39. Annibale Carracci (Italian, 1560–1609), *The Butcher's Shop*, c. 1582. Oil on canvas, 23½ x 28 in. (59.7 x 71 cm). Kimbell Art Museum, Fort Worth. Acquired in 1980

Nevertheless, the Kimbell *Butcher's Shop* remains exceptional for the degree to which Annibale appears to have suppressed his imagination and let reality take over. Beyond the table, our only other serious dispute might be with the butcher on the left, whose pose, as mentioned before, seems stiff and formal, as though influenced by the conventions of aristocratic portraiture. Annibale's proud feelings for butchers could well be part of the explanation. He might have felt inclined, for a variety of personal reasons, to make this butcher look every bit as noble and dignified as the sort of gentleman who normally had himself painted. Still, like the table, the pose is not so egregiously distorted or unnatural as to topple the illusion that Annibale created the painting away from his studio, directly before his subject. As we have seen, this illusion turns on many things, and one yet to be discussed is the painting's free and broken brushwork.

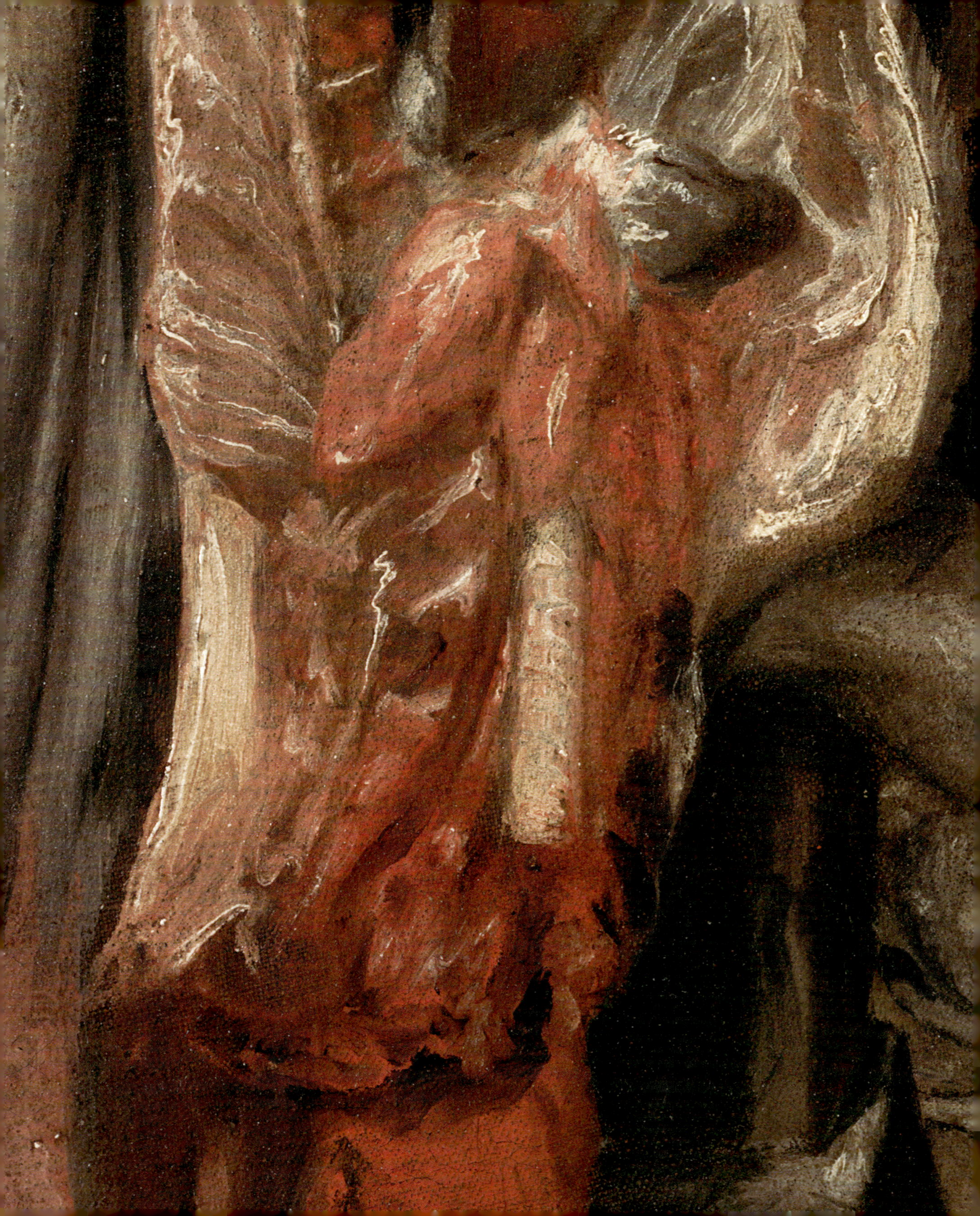

Technique

ONE OF THE MAIN WAYS IN WHICH THE KIMBELL *BUTCHER'S SHOP* RESEMBLES A plein-air painting is in its apparent spontaneity. This arises from a simple fact: any artist attempting a true plein-air painting must work rapidly in order to capture the scene in front of him or her before it changes. The brushwork typically quickens, becoming freer and looser, and this is precisely the style of brushwork that characterizes the Kimbell *Butcher's Shop*. Consider the detail opposite, which shows a section of the hanging carcass on the left. The bolt of white at center is rendered with assurance and flair, and the surrounding reds and whites are applied in short, unhesitating strokes. This seems to go together with the painting's highly naturalistic style, apparent on-location setting, and relatively small dimensions. We might well think that Annibale packed up his painting supplies one day, traveled to a nearby butcher's stall, set up his easel, and proceeded to paint the picture in the course of a morning or an afternoon. If so, we would be almost surely mistaken. As the preceding chapter has suggested, it is virtually certain that Annibale developed the painting in his studio, where he could have labored over its finish as long as he wanted. Why, then, did he choose the style of brushwork he did? All evidence points in one direction: that he sought to increase the impression of directness conveyed by his painting. He wanted it to have all the immediacy of a painting produced on the spot in a single session.

Fig. 40. Annibale Carracci, Kimbell *Butcher's Shop*, detail (see fig. 1)

Before exploring the brushwork in greater detail, it is first helpful to return to the reasons why the Kimbell *Butcher's Shop* is unlikely to have been created outside the studio. The most important is that, before the seventeenth century, there was no tradition in Italy of painting on the spot. The tradition developed fairly rapidly in Rome during the 1610s or 1620s and was almost exclusive to landscape specialists such as Claude Lorrain.[105] Its origins in landscape are understandable in that landscapists needed to go outdoors in order to paint the countryside accurately. Less understandable is why it developed so late. Although beautiful landscapes appear in innumerable Renaissance paintings, no painting produced in Italy before the late sixteenth century features the landscape as its primary subject. The reasons for the slow development of landscape and plein-air painting are complex and need not detain us further. Suffice it to say that before nature could be appreciated for its intrinsic beauty and become worthy of art, the seeds of humanism needed to be sowed and take root, a process that extended over centuries.[106]

If one barrier to plein-air painting was cultural, another was purely pragmatic: painting away from one's studio (especially in public) is a hassle. The artist's equipment must be portable; the elements—whether wind, rain, or the beating sun—could be enormously bothersome; and even if the location were indoors—as with the butcher's complexes in Bologna—there could be jostling crowds, intrusive onlookers, and a general lack of space. Fortunately for artists, *drawing* on location was a far simpler affair, and it is not surprising that plein-air landscape sketches do survive in some numbers from the Renaissance.[107] One of the earliest and most famous is Leonardo da Vinci's *Landscape of the Arno River and Valley* (fig. 41). The sketchy lines suggest an unpremeditated response to nature, and the drawing bears a telling inscription: "on the [feast] of Saint Mary of the Snow, on the day of August 5, 1473" (dì di s[an]ta maria della neve / addj 5 daghossto 1473).[108] Apparently, Leonardo has wandered up into the hills on a holiday, sketchbook in hand, prepared to record various vistas that intrigued him. While he might have been scouting for a good landscape to use in the background of a painting, he was primarily just entertaining himself. He knew that there was no market for landscape paintings and that even if there were, he could not possibly carry all the equipment necessary to paint in that age. To the best of my knowledge, the earliest reference to a portable painting kit being used in Italy dates from 1650.[109]

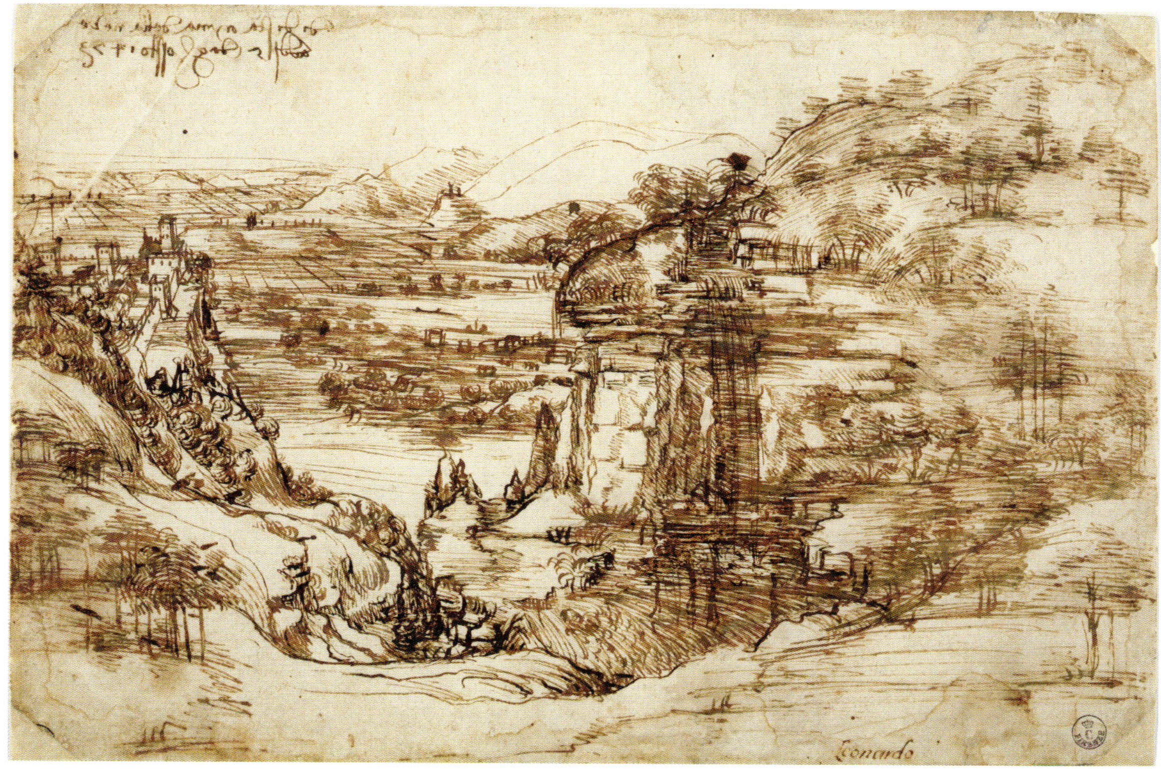

Fig. 41. Leonardo da Vinci (Italian, 1452–1519), *Landscape of the Arno River and Valley*, 1473. Pen and ink drawing, 7½ x 11¼ in. (19 x 28.5 cm). Gabinetto dei Disegni e delle Stampe, Galleria degli Uffizi, Florence

As more and more artists ventured outdoors to sketch, it might be assumed that some would turn their attention to subjects beyond the landscape. In truth, plein-air scenes of everyday life are not prevalent in Italian drawing until Annibale's time.[110] Granted, our view is probably distorted, as such drawings would have been the first to be lost or destroyed, being the least appreciated. But even with as prolific a draftsman as Parmigianino, whose corpus of drawings totals nearly a thousand, only a handful of these can be classified as genre subjects, and how can we be sure that any are plein air? Take, for example, his *Man with a Pregnant Dog,* traditionally dated to the 1530s (fig. 42).[111] The inspiration for the drawing must have come from an observed experience outside his studio, but the draftsmanship is just meticulous enough that we must wonder if Parmigianino did not re-create the scene back in his studio when he had sufficient time for a proper recording.

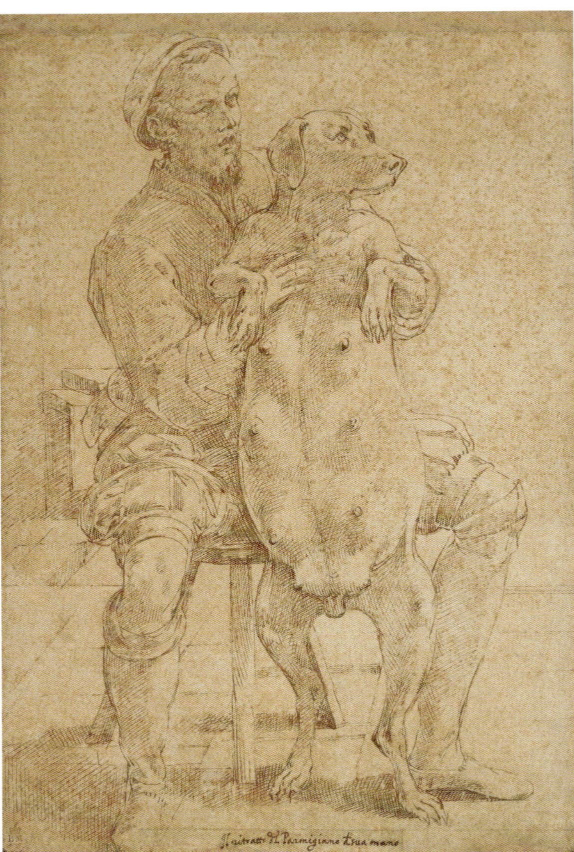

Fig. 42. Parmigianino (Italian, 1503–1540), *Man with a Pregnant Dog*, c. 1524. Brown ink and pen drawing, 12 x 8 in. (30.4 x 20.3 cm). The British Museum, London

Moving forward a half century and focusing on Bologna, the situation is little changed. Among Annibale's immediate predecessors, none were attracted to plein-air drawing, and there are no indications that any of them ever took even the most tentative steps toward *painting* outdoors.[112] If the Kimbell *Butcher's Shop* were plein air, it would have emerged from an almost total art-historical vacuum. Annibale was revolutionary in many ways, but it seems unlikely that he suddenly invented outdoor painting at the age of twenty-two or twenty-three. There is also the issue that while the canvas is small, it is not so small as to be easily portable, unless it was rolled and stretched later.[113] When these observations are combined with the awkward table and the contrived pose of the butcher on the left, the conclusion seems inescapable: while Annibale must have spent long hours preparing for the Kimbell *Butcher's Shop* on the spot, he returned to his studio for the actual painting.

Making things seem other than what they are—a studio painting that looks as if it were done outdoors—was a familiar process for Annibale.[114] His biographer, Carlo Cesare

Malvasia, provides some illuminating anecdotes in this regard. In one, he relates how Annibale was fond of teasing his cook (and cat) with illusionistically painted pieces of meat.[115] In another, we learn that he joined his cousin and brother in devising a famous series of pictorial guessing games that were meant to play on the viewer's perception of reality.[116] An example, illustrated below (fig. 43), is supposed to represent a mason; the top of the mason's head and trowel poke just above the wall he is working on. Illusionism was central to Annibale's art, and he was fully aware that two paintings of the same subject could invite totally different responses depending on how they were painted. The tighter the brushwork, the more labored and artificial the subject looked; the quicker the brushwork, the more spontaneous and lifelike. It was an easy choice for the young Annibale.

Did Annibale's desire to create the most lifelike genre paintings possible lead to his decision to invent a new style of brushwork for himself? According to the available evidence, his train of thought ran in a somewhat opposite direction. His preference for summary brushwork and thickly applied paint seems to have come at least a year or two before any of his major genre paintings, including the Kimbell's. One source is likely to have been Passarotti, whose Rome *Butcher's Shop* exhibits considerable rawness in its paint application (fig. 44). What is striking about Passarotti is that he tended to limit this technique to his genre paintings, as though rough brushwork was only appropriate for rough subjects. His portraits and religious paintings are much more polished in their technique, as was the standard in Bologna.

Tight brushwork was not, however, the standard in Venice, which Annibale appears to have visited for the first time around 1580.[117] On seeing the great masterpieces of Titian,

Fig. 43. Carlo Cesare Malvasia, a pictorial riddle depicting a mason working on a wall, after the Carracci. From Malvasia's *Felsina pittrice: vite de' pittori bolognesi* (Bologna, 1678)

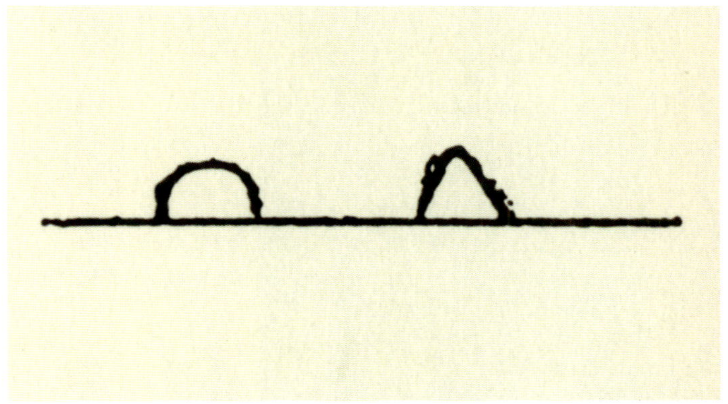

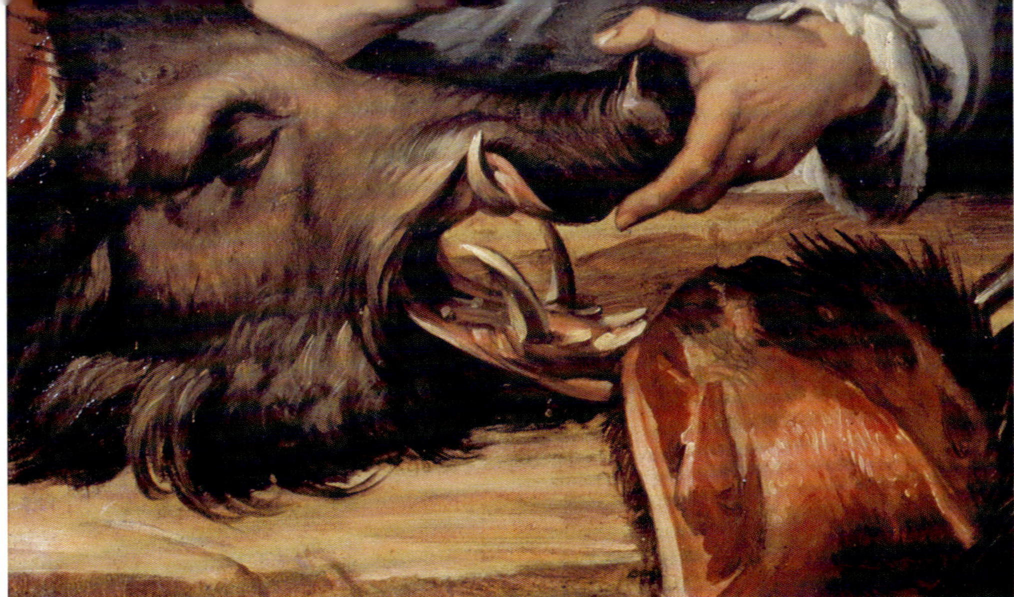

Fig. 44. Bartolomeo Passarotti, *The Butcher's Shop*, detail (see fig. 16)

Tintoretto, and Veronese, he would have known instantly that he must give more thought to how he handled paint. The lesson of these artists was that *colorito* (coloring) should be given priority over *disegno* (drawing) when creating a painting.[118] Annibale had grown up in a culture that espoused the opposite view, that colorito was secondary and that painters should focus on perfect compositions and apply their paint in a meticulous, highly controlled way. If Annibale had not already begun to doubt this approach before going to Venice, a few weeks in the Serenissima would have done the job. Its churches, palaces, and *scuole*, or lay confraternities, were full of exquisite reminders that painting should be about paint—how pigments are laid, how they are blended, and how they can be built up to form broken surfaces that catch the light.

No secure facts are known about Annibale's first trip to Venice, but it can be reasonably hypothesized which paintings he saw. In the main, these would have been the ones in the city's major churches and included such exhilarating essays in loosely and thickly applied paint as Titian's *Annunciation* in San Salvador (fig. 45).[119] Its technique is typically Venetian and closely parallels that of the Kimbell *Butcher's Shop*. Like all great Venetian painters active from the early sixteenth century on, Titian began the *Annunciation* by applying a light gray or brown ground to his canvas.[120] On top, he likely blocked out the basic outlines of his

Opposite page: **Fig. 45.** Titian (Italian, c. 1488–1576), *The Annunciation*, 1559–62. Oil on canvas, 158¾ x 92½ in. (403 x 235 cm). Church of San Salvador, Venice

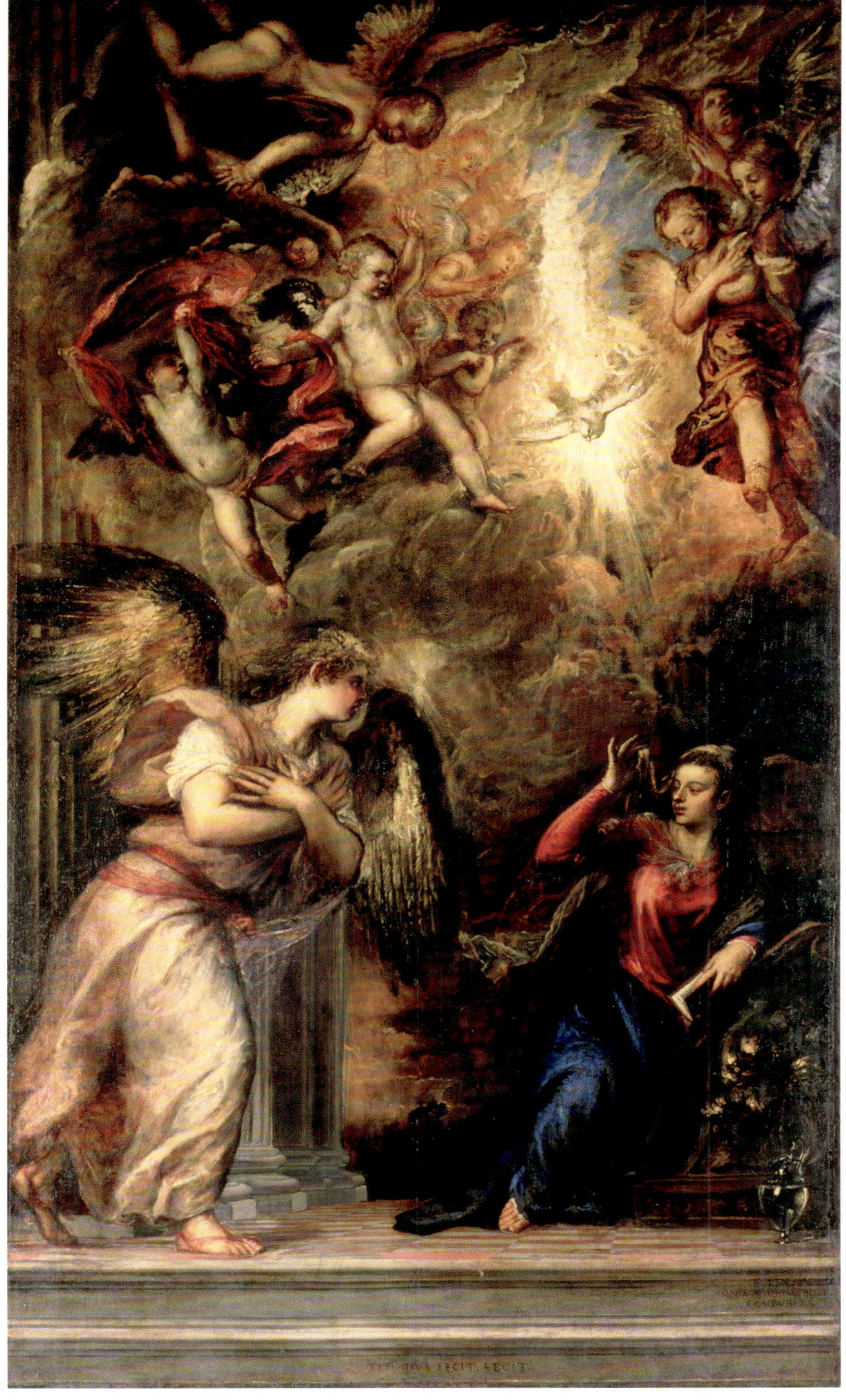

composition in dark paint, perhaps consulting a cartoon, or full-scale preparatory drawing. Once this had been accomplished, it was time for the actual painting. The pigments and glazes would have been applied layer by layer in order of increasing brightness. The whites were often saved for the last, which helps to explain why they are typically among the thickest, or most richly impasted, on a sixteenth-century Venetian painting. One advantage of the layering process is that edits were easy to make. If a section needed correcting, it was simply painted over. This bred confidence and encouraged Titian and his contemporaries to let their brushes move with absolute freedom and energy. Consider a detail such as the furl of drapery held by the bunch of angels in the center left of Titian's *Annunciation* (fig. 46). From afar, this passage reads coherently, and our main impression is that the forms have a flickering quality that makes the fabric look pliable, satiny, and on the move. Up close, we

Fig. 46. Titian, *The Annunciation*, detail (see fig. 45)

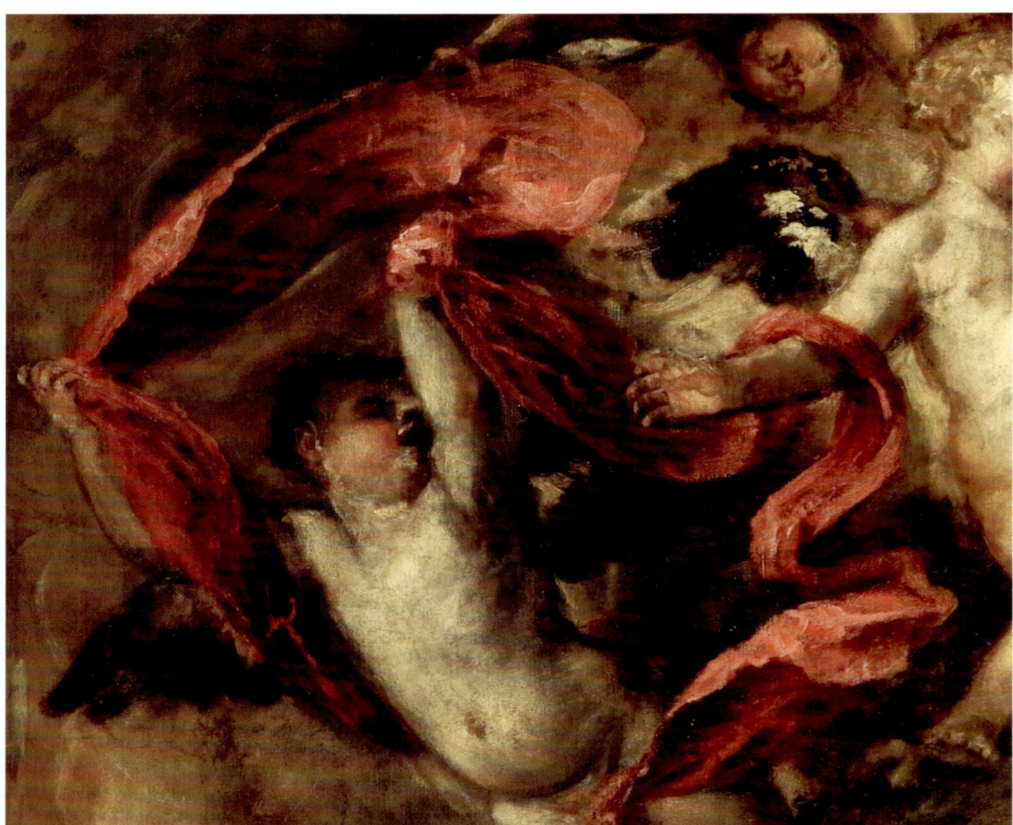

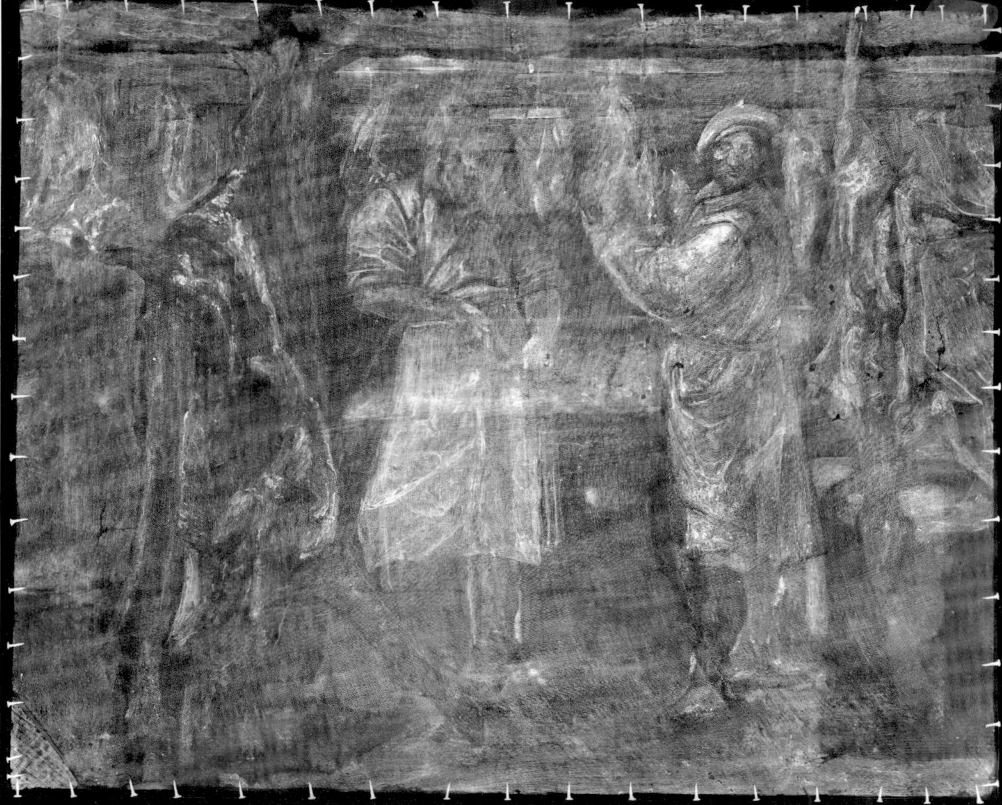

Fig. 47. X-radiograph of the Kimbell *Butcher's Shop*

face something totally different, a tussle of broad strokes of white pigments and pinkish and red glazes that, with their flowing turns, sudden crisscrosses, and graceful taperings, convey the joy Titian felt when handling a loaded brush.

At no point in his career did Annibale ever reach the same levels of visceral paint application as the mature Titian. But we still cannot help but marvel at the performance he delivered with the Kimbell *Butcher's Shop*. It is masterfully Venetian in its technique, and this is not only true of the brushwork. From the start, Annibale approached the painting in a typically Venetian way, choosing a light brown ground. He then proceeded as Titian, Tintoretto, or Veronese might, by allowing his composition to unfold as he proceeded, building up the paint one layer at a time (sometimes with considerable periods of drying between them). The improvisatory nature of his approach is readily demonstrated by the butcher on the left, who was added on top of the table. This is visible to the naked eye and can also be appreciated in the X-radiograph (fig. 47).[121] The hanging pieces of meat on the

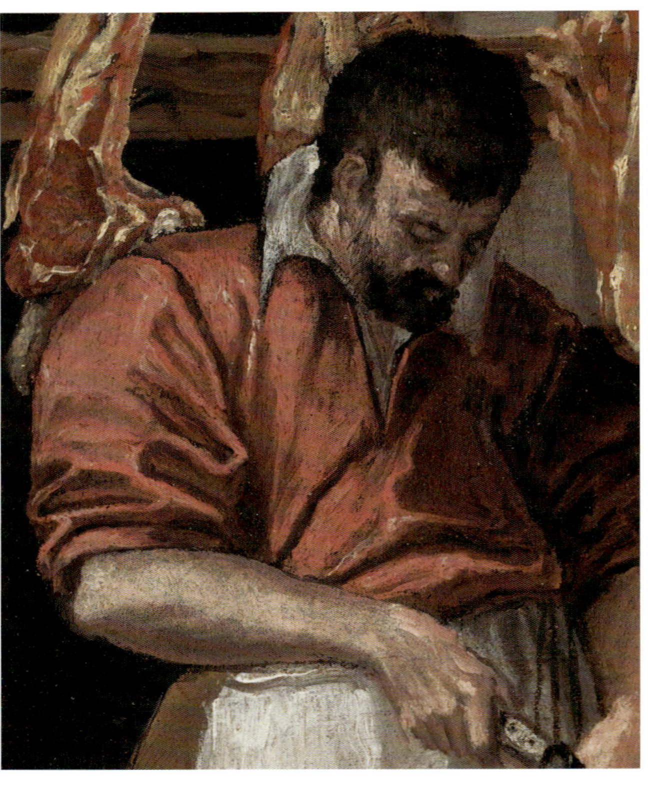

Fig. 48. Annibale Carracci, Kimbell *Butcher's Shop*, detail (see fig. 1)

back rafter were also painted over completed forms. The fact that these changes are obvious in the X-radiograph indicates that Annibale let some time (likely days or maybe even weeks) pass between painting sessions. Otherwise, the paint would not have had sufficient time to dry, and the pigments would look more like they do nearly everywhere else in the painting: wet-in-wet, the term for when pigments are applied directly on top of other pigments and allowed to mix.

Throughout Annibale's trial-and-error process of arriving at his composition, he remained singularly focused on his style of brushwork, insisting that it be sketchy, expressive, and Venetian. We have already considered one detail that makes this point, the lower portion of the carcass on the left (fig. 40). Moving to another, the right sleeve of the butcher holding a knife, we are struck by Venetian parallels that are equally strong (fig. 48). Particularly Venetian is the palette and the way it subtly gradates between deep burgundy, red, pink, and

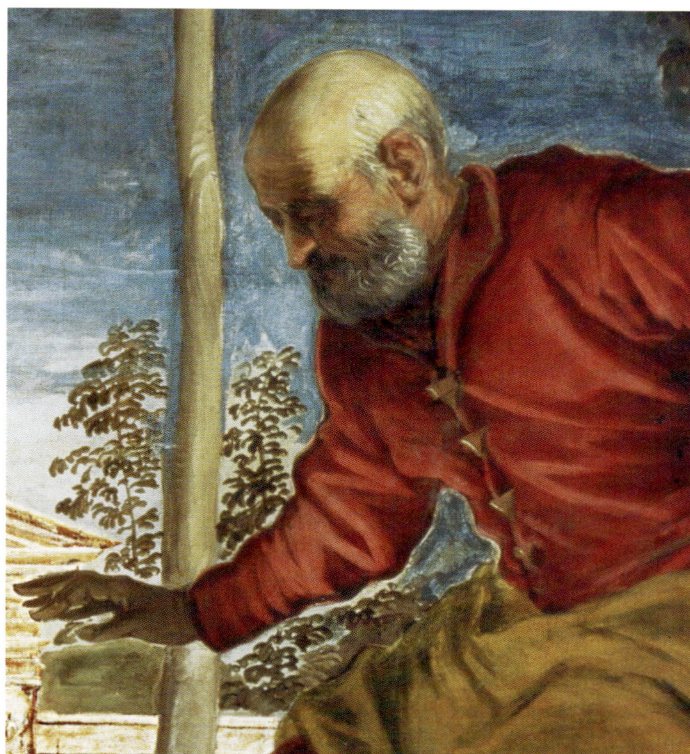

Fig. 49. Jacopo Tintoretto (Italian, 1519–1594), *The Miracle of Saint Mark Freeing the Slave* (detail), 1548, oil on canvas. Galleria dell'Accademia, Venice

pinkish white. We find the same chromatic shift in many places in Titian's aforementioned *Annunciation* (fig. 45), although it could well have been Tintoretto, Veronese, or even the lesser-known Jacopo Bassano who exerted the stronger influence in this regard. This is suggested by any number of works, including Tintoretto's *Miracle of the Slave,* which Annibale could well have seen in 1580.[122] The right sleeve of an onlooker presents one of the best comparisons (fig. 49). The similarities in color are obvious, but so too the zigzagging pattern used in both works to suggest bunched fabric. Like Tintoretto, Annibale has built up his reds from dark to light, finishing the forward edge of the sleeve with several meandering strokes that, in their gentle sweeps and occasional abrupt turns, celebrate their creator's extraordinarily nimble and efficient touch.

In terms of technique and style of brushwork, the Kimbell *Butcher's Shop* is by no means unique in Annibale's oeuvre. The Oxford *Butcher's Shop* is decidedly Venetian in its

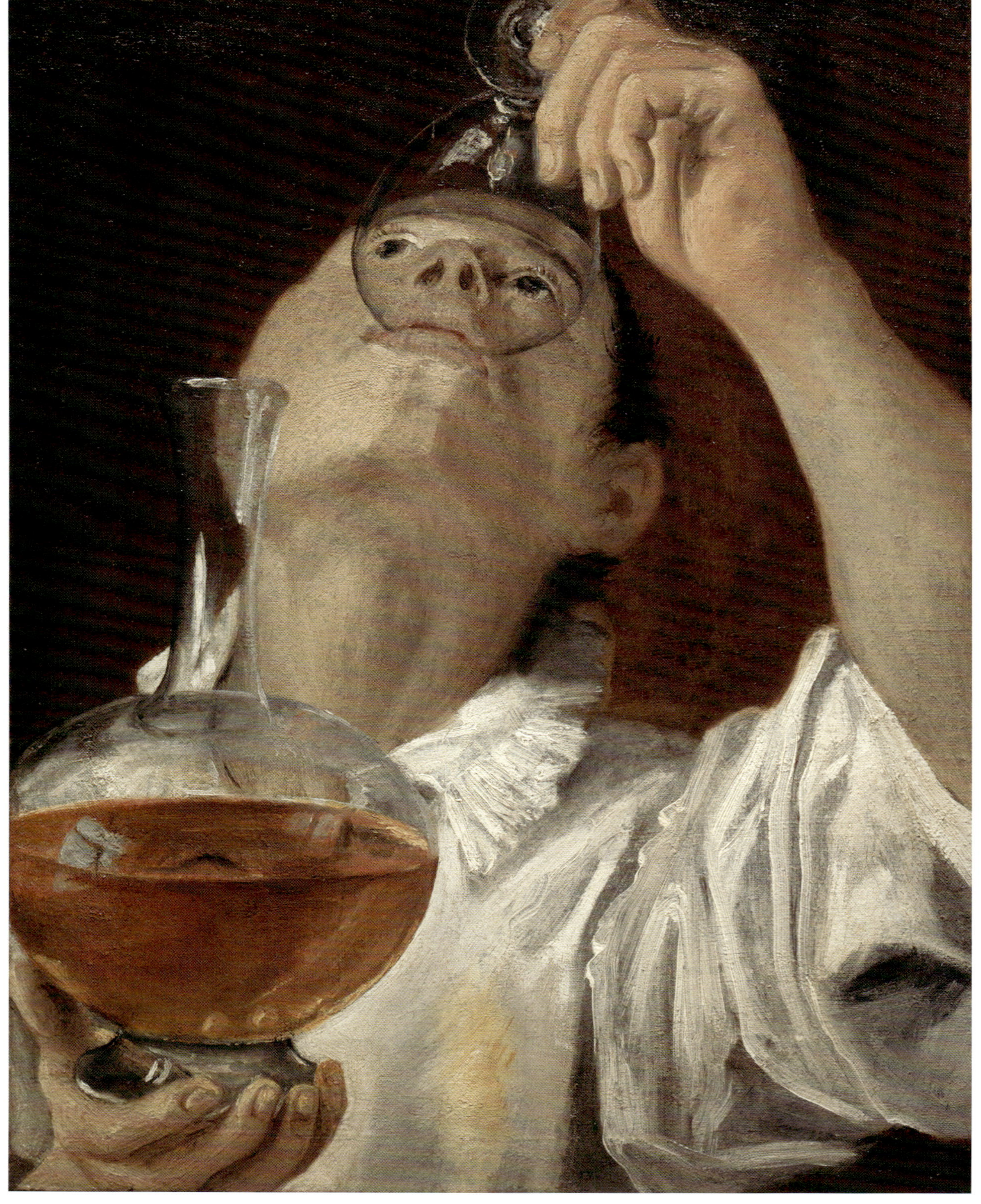

approach, and the same can be said for his other genre paintings of the early 1580s, including *Boy Drinking* in the Cleveland Museum of Art (fig. 50).[123] This second work is an especially good example for the vigorous and thick brushwork that makes up the boy's left sleeve. This painting is also instructive because it emphasizes the relationship that Annibale perceived between direct observation, spontaneity, and spirited paint handling. In *Boy Drinking*, he was not only concerned with the challenging pose and the difficulties presented by the reflections in the glass and the half-filled decanter. He was also committed to understanding how to convey the impression of a live model captured at a specific moment in time. His solution was the same plein-air illusionism that distinguishes the Kimbell *Butcher's Shop*. He knew that he must try to make his painting look as though it had been conceived at the moment inspiration struck. Logic dictated that he could not be slavish in his finish, although he must have quickly realized that it was not simply a matter of increasing the speed at which he applied the paint to his canvas. His brushwork needed to be efficient and expressive, and there was no better model than the Venetians, who would have instilled in him the necessary confidence to break with local tradition and to turn a painting about the everyday into a painting about the experience of seeing the everyday. This is the brilliance of the Kimbell *Butcher's Shop*.

Fig. 50. Annibale Carracci (Italian, 1560–1609), *Boy Drinking*, c. 1582–83. Oil on canvas, 22 x 17¼ in. (55.8 x 43.7 cm). The Cleveland Museum of Art. Leonard C. Hanna, Jr. Fund, 1994.4

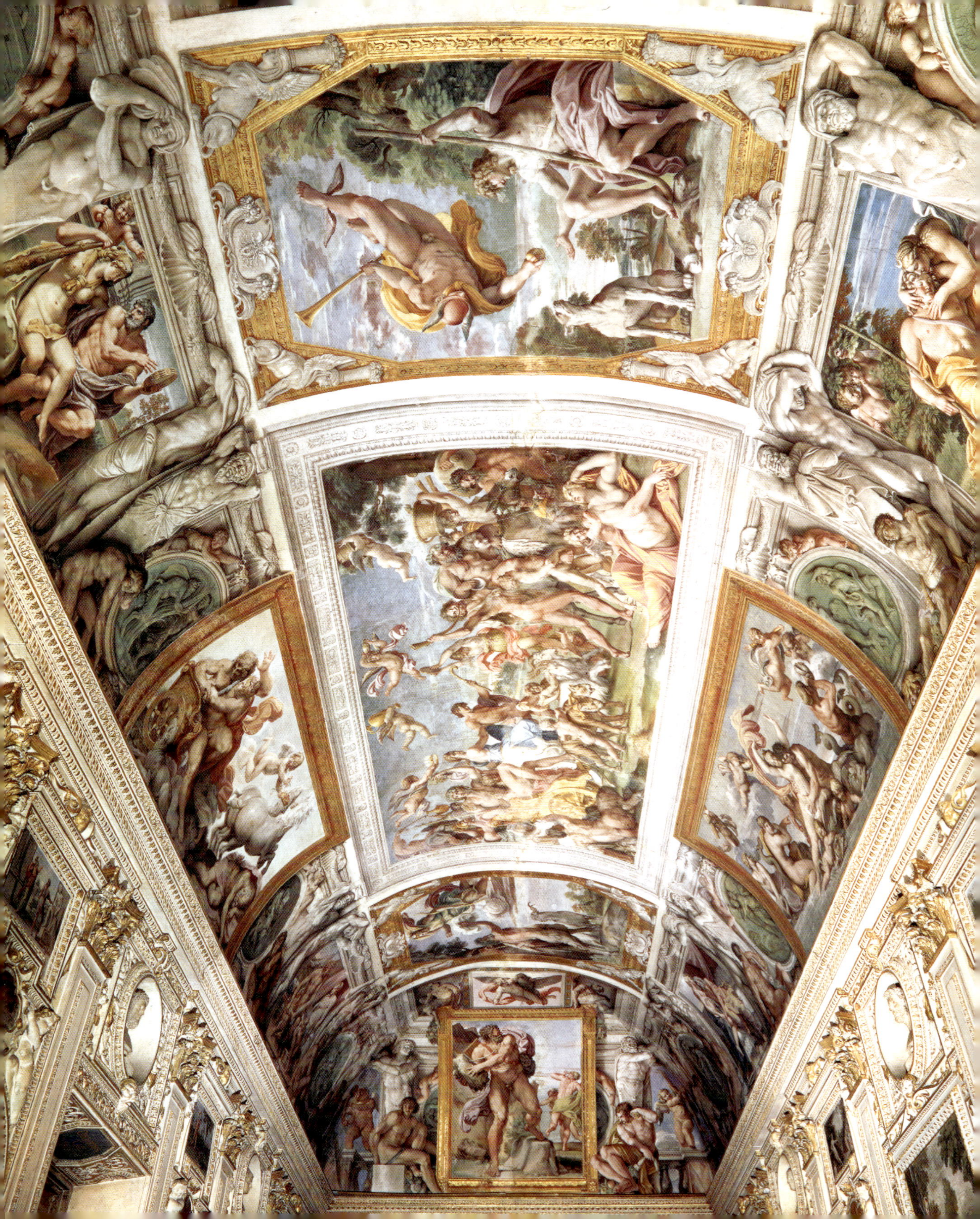

From *The Butcher's Shop* to the Future of Painting

S ANNIBALE WAS APPLYING THE FINAL TOUCHES OF PAINT TO THE KIMBELL *Butcher's Shop*, he could hardly have imagined that in less than twenty years he would be standing on scaffolds in one of the grandest palaces in all of Rome, the Palazzo Farnese, engaged on a cycle of frescoes that would seal his reputation for posterity as one of the fathers of Baroque art (fig. 51). Given all that has been said about the revolutionary quality of his genre paintings, one might expect his rise to stardom to have come about through a similar formula of naturalism. The truth, however, is otherwise. During the roughly fifteen years between the Kimbell *Butcher's Shop* and the Farnese Gallery, Annibale remade himself as an artist, and the Annibale who came to be immortalized was the one who could paint such beautifully idealized figures as the triumphal Bacchus and Ariadne in the central scene on the Gallery's vault (fig. 52). To Giovanni Pietro Bellori, one of his earliest biographers, Annibale was great for one simple reason: he possessed the phenomenal ability to look at ancient sculpture and to create art of equal perfection, an achievement not realized in Italian art since Raphael.[124] The "crude" genre paintings of Annibale's youth distracted from this image, and Bellori chose not to mention any in his text. Today, the genre paintings are rightly celebrated as one of the main foundations of Annibale's mature style. If not for them, he is unlikely to have developed the mastery to make figures such as the Bacchus and Ariadne look so vital and alive.

Fig. 51. Annibale Carracci (Italian, 1560–1609), Farnese Gallery, 1597/98–1608, fresco. Palazzo Farnese, Rome

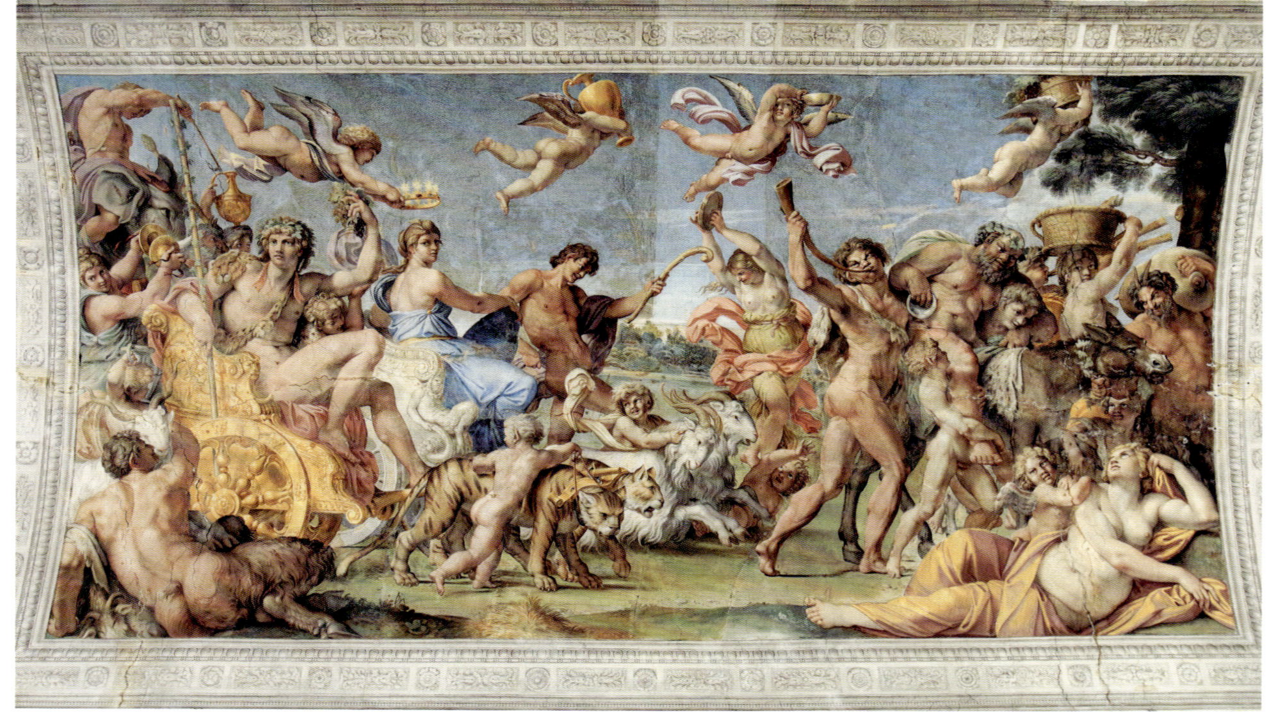

Fig. 52. Annibale Carracci, *The Triumph of Bacchus and Ariadne*, 1597/98–1601, fresco. Farnese Gallery, Palazzo Farnese, Rome

The route Annibale took to his mature style passed through multiple stages. In the first, he drew from the lessons of genre painting, privileging direct presentation, vigorous naturalism, and rough brushwork. To the surprise of many, this was the mode in which he carried out his first public work, the *Crucifixion* now in Santa Maria della Carità, unveiled in 1583 (fig. 53).[125] As Malvasia reports, it was instantly criticized for being too much like a genre painting. The main complaint was that Annibale had done little more than to arrange a group of life studies on his canvas, and it confounded older artists such as Passarotti as to why he would include such indecorous, genrelike details as the view of Saint Dominic's dirty feet.[126] It should be noted that the *Crucifixion* holds special importance for the Kimbell *Butcher's Shop* in that, as the earliest documented work by Annibale, it provides an essential guidepost for dating. The two paintings are usually thought to be roughly coeval, although *The Butcher's Shop* could

Fig. 53. Annibale Carracci (Italian, 1560–1609), *The Crucifixion*, 1583. Oil on canvas, 120 x 82⅜ in. (305 x 210 cm). Church of Santa Maria della Carità, Bologna

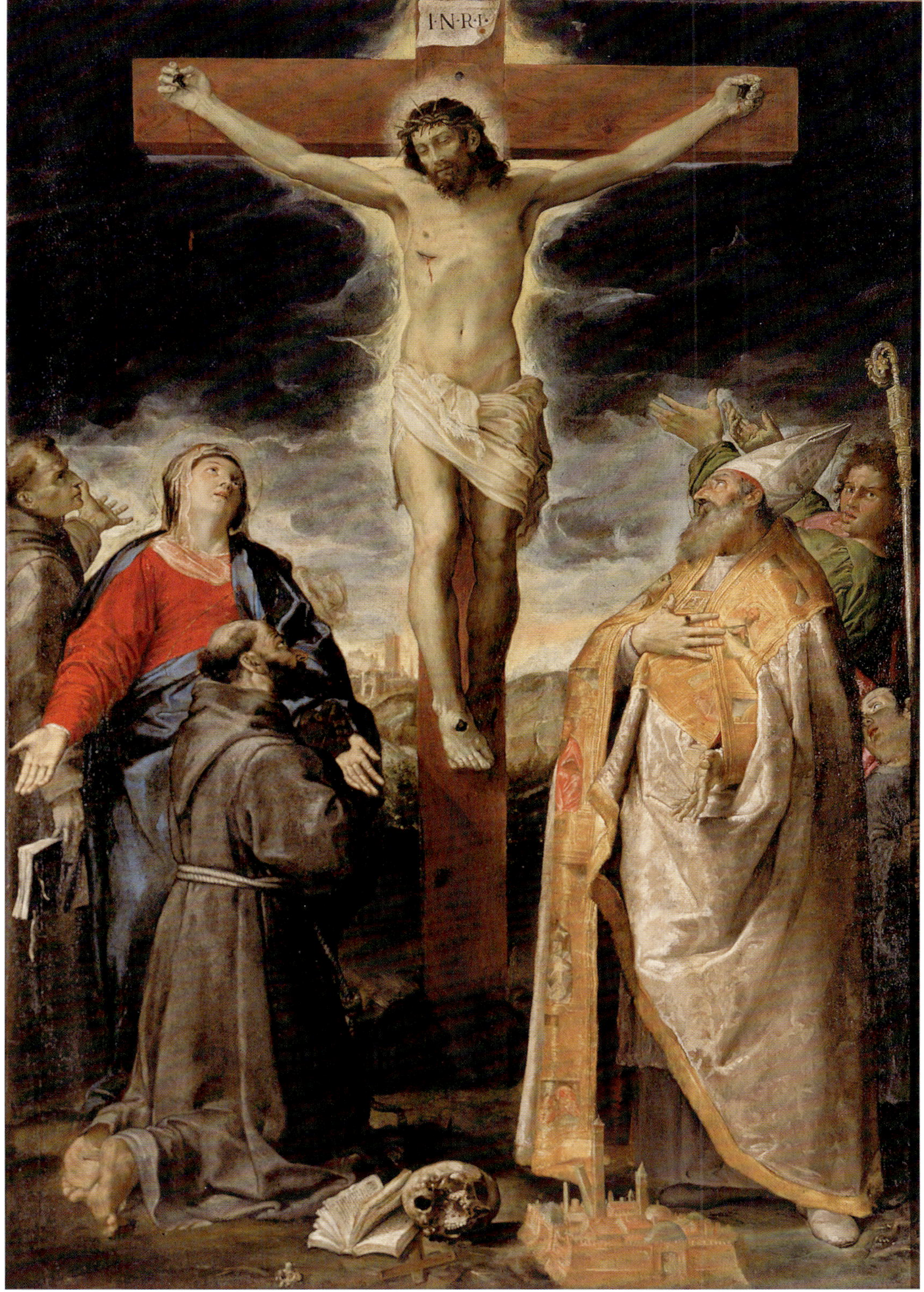

well date from early 1582—or even late 1581, just after Annibale's probable return from Venice. It is unlikely to be later than 1583: the criticisms of the *Crucifixion* that year appear to have resonated with Annibale, who began to change his style almost immediately. His next altarpiece, executed between 1583 and 1585, is a work of much softer figures and greater compositional grace: the aforementioned *Baptism of Christ* for the Canobbi chapel in Santi Gregorio e Siro (fig. 29).[127] Gone is the earthiness of the *Crucifixion*, replaced by an elegance and ethereality that can be attributed to Annibale's discovery of Correggio and Federico Barocci. As Annibale progressed through the next decade, he turned repeatedly to these two artists for inspiration, in addition to the Venetian masters Titian, Tintoretto, and Veronese. At different times, different influences predominated, as he was constantly searching for the perfect combination of styles. His overarching concern was that his paintings make a direct appeal to the viewer's emotions, and he knew that success was a delicate balancing act, involving decisions about light, color, gesture, composition, and so forth.[128]

Despite the stylistic diversity of Annibale's pre-Roman paintings, there were important constants. Annibale recognized that for a painting to be believable, it had to be comprehensible, and he always worked hard to develop rational spaces that were not tightly packed with bodies, as was the custom of the Mannerists. The second important constant in his art was also born of his concern for pictorial believability. As he had learned from his genre paintings, the illusion of reality was instantly shattered if any of the figures moved or gestured in ways not conforming to reality. To safeguard against this possibility, he swore himself to life study, and there is no shortage of evidence among his drawings. A beautiful example is his study in the Musée du Louvre, Paris, for the boy taking off his shirt in the lower left of the *Baptism* (figs. 54, 55).[129] While the drawing does not correspond precisely to the painted figure, it makes the important point that in preparing for his paintings, Annibale relied heavily on studio models, whom he posed according to the demands of the composition and drew from various angles.[130]

The high place Annibale reserved for life study in his artistic process becomes even clearer when we address the Carracci Academy. Shortly after returning to Bologna from their travels in northern Italy around 1582, Annibale, Agostino, and Ludovico founded an arts academy where they could explore their ideas about art and teach their approach to others.[131] The first gatherings were held at Ludovico's studio, and in addition to instituting an ambitious

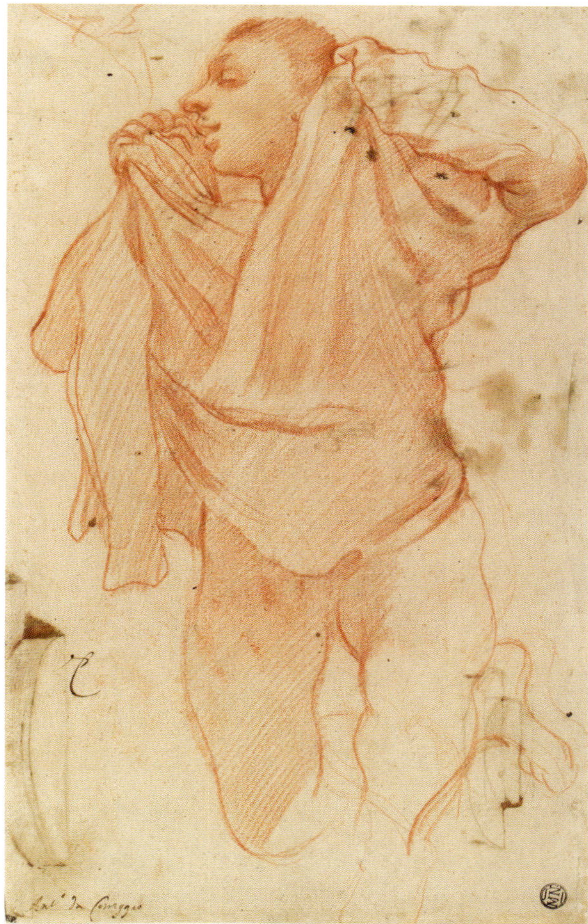
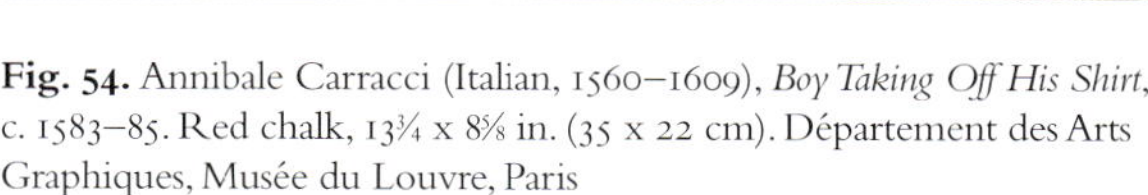

Fig. 54. Annibale Carracci (Italian, 1560–1609), *Boy Taking Off His Shirt*, c. 1583–85. Red chalk, 13¾ x 8⅝ in. (35 x 22 cm). Département des Arts Graphiques, Musée du Louvre, Paris

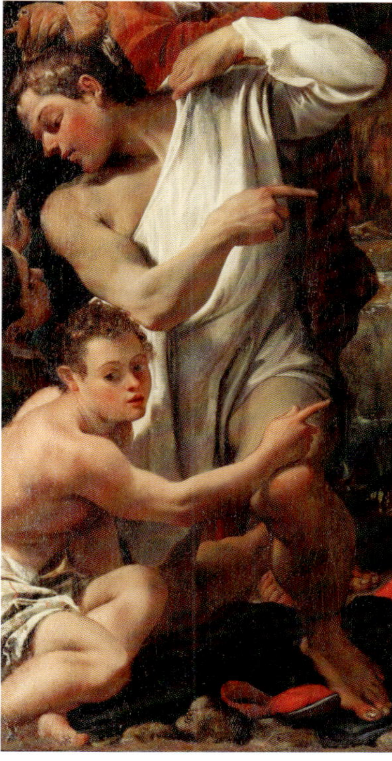

Fig. 55. Annibale Carracci, *The Baptism of Christ*, detail (see fig. 29)

program of intellectual study, the Carracci determined that life drawing should be given an unprecedentedly large role in the curriculum.[132] A typical drawing session saw students, including the Carracci themselves, seated around a nude model who would be asked to hold different poses for extended periods.[133] The resulting studies, called "academies" after the Carracci practice, survive in great numbers, and many—especially Annibale's—show an astonishing respect for the subtleties of human flesh, the intricacies of human form.[134] When models were not available, the Carracci and their pupils turned their attention to the everyday and also drew one another.[135] The Carracci knew that before an artist could accept life study as

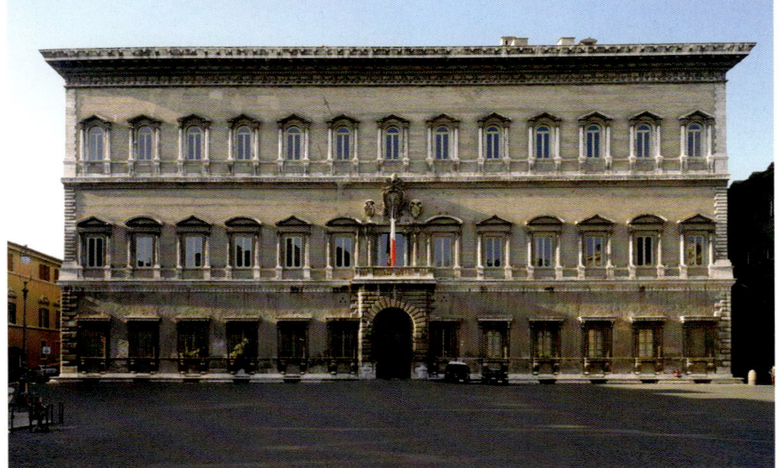

Fig. 56. Antonio da Sangallo the Younger (Italian, 1484–1546) and Michelangelo Buonarroti (Italian, 1475–1564), Palazzo Farnese, Rome, 1517–46

a core component of his or her preparatory procedures, it had to become second nature, and this required long hours of practice over many years. Annibale put himself through this training with extraordinary diligence, and it became ingrained in him that the arts of painting and life study were integrally connected. This was not an approach that he was willing to abandon on a whim, and the proof is that he continued to subscribe to it even after his move to Rome.

In the fall of 1594, Annibale arrived in the Eternal City, invited by Cardinal Odoardo Farnese, who sought a painter to fresco the main salon in his family's palace (fig. 56).[136] The salon project ended up being postponed, and Annibale was assigned two different rooms, the later one being the renowned Farnese Gallery, executed between 1597 and 1601, just eight years before his death, in 1609 (see figs. 2, 51, 52).[137] During the several years leading up to the commission, he was busy taking stock of his new artistic environment and trying to determine how best to respond. Understandably, Michelangelo and Raphael weighed heavily on his mind, and he became more and more receptive to their styles. Ancient sculpture also exerted an enormous pull; he knew it underlay Michelangelo's and Raphael's art and had to be learned completely. His figures gained in monumentality; their outlines became firmer; and he placed new emphasis on compositional structure. He would not fully adopt a Roman style, however, until he began work on the Gallery, and one of the reasons for the wait is that no earlier project had forced him to come to grips with Michelangelo's Sistine Ceiling so completely.[138] He greatly admired Michelangelo's ceiling for its logic and stability and determined that it should be one of the principal models for the system of illusionistic vaulting that he would deploy in the Gallery.[139] He simultaneously recognized that if his decorations were to match Michelangelo's in presence and vigor, they must be stylistically unified, which meant that the figures in the pictorial fields had to convey the same mass and sculptural quality as those comprising the frames. This—combined with the fact that the Gallery was to house important specimens from the Farnese family's stunning collection of ancient sculptures—compelled Annibale to move unflinchingly toward a pure Roman style, and among the clearest indications is his figure of Polyphemus on the north end of the vault (fig. 57). The angry giant, who prepares to hurl a boulder at his rival Acis, is unmistakably Roman—and not just superficially. His hulking physique, powerful movement, violent expression, and tight execution are masterfully integrated and demonstrate a complete fluency on the part of Annibale in the complementary languages of ancient and High Renaissance art.

To look at the Polyphemus casually, however, is to think that Annibale, in remaking his style, became singularly focused on the chiseled bodies and perfect complexions of ancient sculptures such as the *Torso Belvedere* (fig. 58), a possible starting point for the Polyphemus. So striking are the similarities that we cannot help but ask if Annibale's new method was not simply to study the best ancient sculptures available to him in Rome and to imagine how they might look fully restored and in paint. By now, it should be obvious that Annibale was never one to favor such straightforward solutions. The Polyphemus draws from ancient sculpture in many important ways, but it is not for its idealization that the figure is so convincing.[140] We stand in awe of it for its naturalism. Consider the pose. To generate the necessary speed to launch a boulder of that size, a real human would need to be absolutely balanced, with one foot planted firmly on the ground to counteract the considerable force generated by his or her torso as it uncoiled. In the painting, Annibale demonstrates a complete grasp of these physics, and even if Polyphemus may look unreal for his bulging musculature, he becomes real to us because he moves in accordance with the same laws of nature to which we are bound.[141] Suddenly, the ideal seems real, a feat of artistry that Annibale was almost uniquely qualified to achieve. With the exception of the other great naturalist of the period, Caravaggio, no artist in Rome was as committed to life study as Annibale, and if there was a secret ingredient to his frescoes in the Gallery, this was it. As many of his

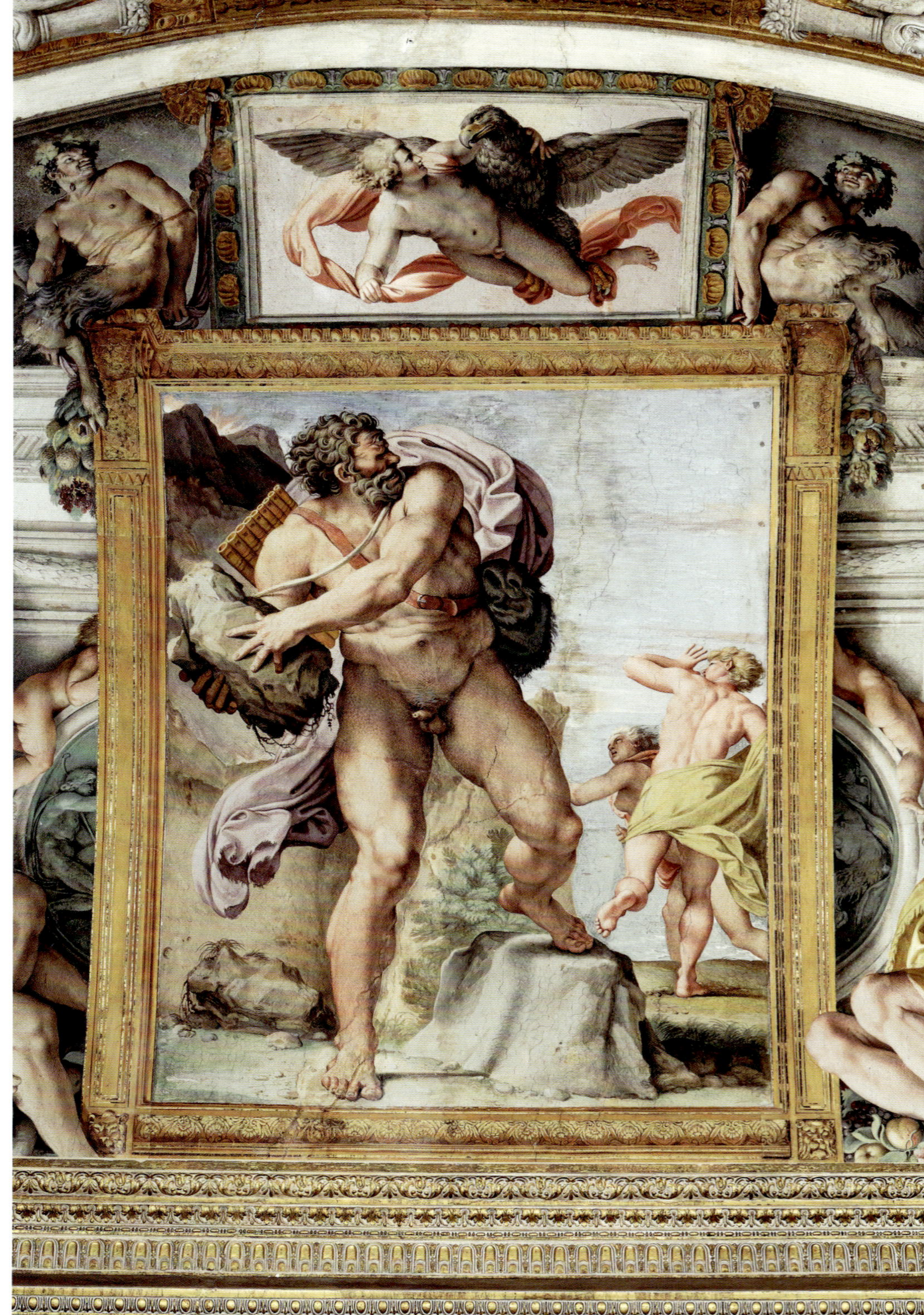

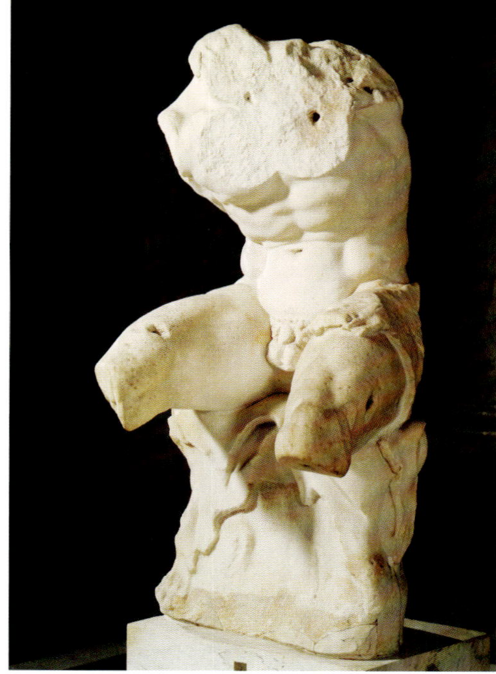

Opposite page:
Fig. 57. Annibale Carracci (Italian, 1560–1609), *Polyphemus and Acis*, 1597/98–1601, fresco. Farnese Gallery, Palazzo Farnese, Rome

Fig. 58. Apollonios of Athens (Greek, 1st century BC), *Belvedere Torso*, 1st century BC. Marble, h. 62⅝ in. (159 cm). Museo Pio Clementino, Vatican Museums, Vatican City

preparatory drawings for the Gallery attest, a figure was not ready to be painted until it had undergone a careful process of review based on life study.[142] Some figures evolved directly from live models, while others were perfected at later stages with drawings from life. Not since Raphael had an artist managed to chart as perfect a course between ancient art and nature, and the praise—including the following encomium by Bellori—was instant and profound: "Oh Rome, well may you glory in the genius and the skill of Annibale, for it was by his merit that the golden age of painting was revived in you."[143]

How humbly this revolution had begun. Today, wandering the galleries of the Kimbell Art Museum, visitors often have a difficult time fathoming how Annibale's modestly scaled *Butcher's Shop* could have been a milestone in the revival of High Renaissance art. This revival is now considered one of the seminal events in the birth of the stylistic movement known as the Baroque. It pays to remember that if Annibale had not undertaken genre paintings such as the Kimbell *Butcher's Shop*, he never would have developed the instincts to look at ancient sculpture and to consider how it might be improved through life study. The Farnese Gallery would not be what it is, and many of the greatest artists of the Baroque— from Peter Paul Rubens to Gianlorenzo Bernini—would have been robbed of essential inspiration. The Kimbell *Butcher's Shop* not only presaged the future of painting; it helped to lay its foundation.

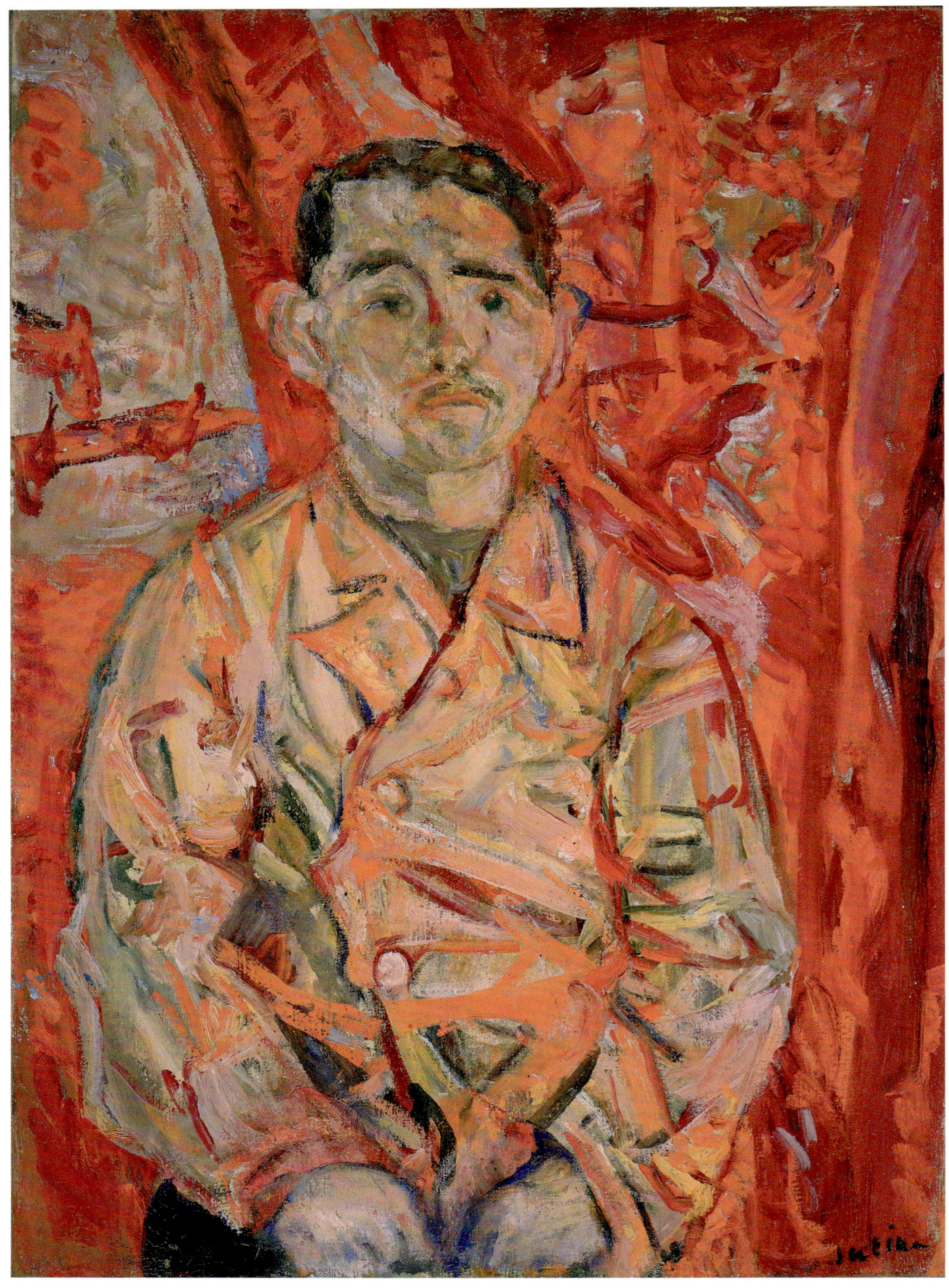

Postscript

The *Butcher's Shop* entered the Kimbell's collection in 1980. It was among the first paintings proposed for acquisition by the Museum's second director, the late Edmund P. Pillsbury, who contributed to the formation of one of the finest collections of Italian Baroque art in the United States. As Pillsbury shared with me several weeks before his death, he admired *The Butcher's Shop* for its considerable modernity and was fond of the way it sometimes fooled even knowledgeable viewers into assuming it was painted much later than it was. *The Butcher's Shop* anticipates important aspects of eighteenth- and nineteenth-century French painting—whether Jean-Siméon Chardin or Gustave Courbet—and the parallels in approach continue even later, as with Chaïm Soutine and paintings such as his *Butcher Boy*, whose direct presentation, honest subject, and lively manner would surely have impressed the young Annibale (fig. 59).

Fig. 59. Chaïm Soutine (Russian, 1893–1943), *The Butcher Boy*, c. 1919. Oil on canvas, 27½ x 19½ in. (69.9 x 49.5 cm). Private collection

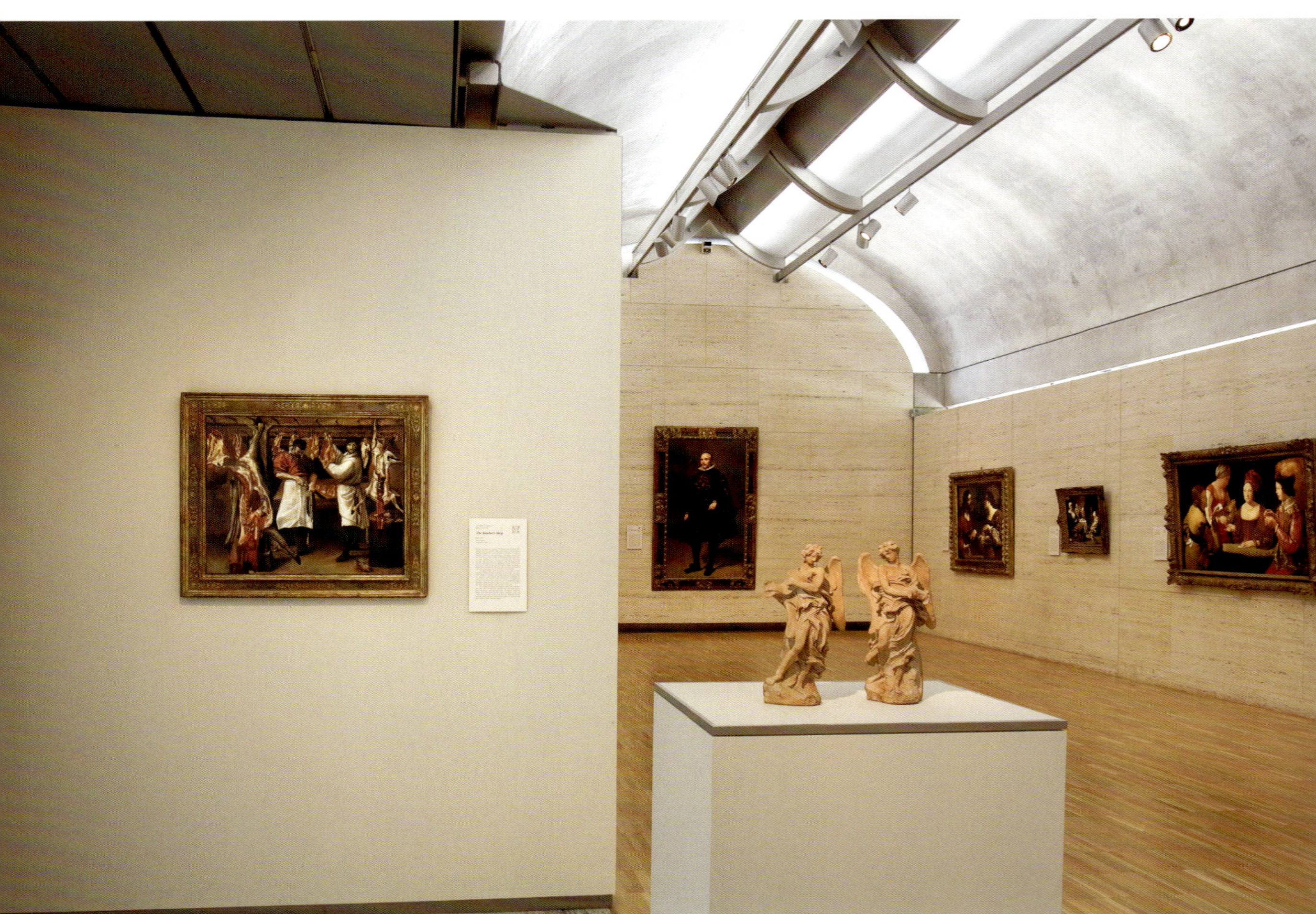

Fig. 60. South gallery with *The Butcher's Shop*, Kimbell Art Museum, Fort Worth, 2010

Acknowledgments

I F THIS BOOK PROVIDES ONE LASTING MEMORY FOR ME, IT WILL BE THE WEEK I SPENT IN Bologna during March 2010 following in the footsteps of Annibale and his butchers. The city was unfailingly generous in its help, and I extend a warm thanks to Pierangelo Bellettini, Piero Cammarota, Mario Fanti, and Daniele Schiavina. Of all my new colleagues in Bologna, however, three deserve special mention, as the book would be infinitely less rich without their photographic contributions: Giuseppe Nicoletti and Elena Drudi of Studio Pym and Corinna Giudici of the Archivio Fotografico della Soprintendenza. Each worked long hours to ensure that I had all the necessary photographs to tell the story of *The Butcher's Shop* properly and beautifully.

Closer to the Kimbell Art Museum, there are many individuals who provided help during various stages of the project. I am grateful to Virginia Brilliant, Karen Serres, Mary Vaccaro, and Kimbell deputy director Malcolm Warner for reading drafts of the book—the last for reading *two* drafts. The Kimbell's chief conservator, Claire Barry, and assistant conservator, Bart Devolder, were enormously helpful in reviewing the chapter on technique and suggesting ways I could improve it. My research also benefited from conversations with Niall Atkinson, Douglas Biow, Philip Haas, Frederick Ilchman, and Edmund P. Pillsbury. The Kimbell's chief librarian, Chia-Chun Shih, saw to it that I was never without the library materials I needed, and Steven Gassett is to be thanked for his efficient service in the department of interlibrary loans. The editing and production of the book were overseen by the Kimbell's manager of publications, Wendy P. Gottlieb, who brought her customary professionalism to the task, and we are both indebted to publications and editorial assistant Megan Smyth for her diligence as a proofreader and her patient handling of the photographs. Tom Dawson is to be commended for another superb design in the Kimbell Masterpiece Series. Finally, I thank the Kimbell's director, Eric M. Lee, for his enthusiastic support.

C. D. D.

1. For the provenance of the Oxford *Butcher's Shop*, see Byam Shaw 1967, p. 100; and Posner 1971, vol. 2, pp. 3–4.
2. Millar 1970–72, p. 186.
3. Lapenta and Morselli 2006, p. 325.
4. One hypothesis is that it came to Mantua in 1621, when Ferdinando Gonzaga acquired the collection of Carlo Mangino, a Bolognese goldsmith. See Zapperi 1989, p. 67, n. 23; Rossi 1997, p. 21; and Furlotti 2000, pp. 50–51.
5. The complete provenance of the Kimbell *Butcher's Shop* is as follows: John Campbell Hamilton-Gordon, 7th Earl of Haddo and 1st Marquess of Aberdeen and Temair, Haddo House, Aberdeenshire, Scotland; by descent to his grandson, Maj. David George Ian Alexander Gordon, 4th Marquess of Aberdeen and Temair, Haddo House, Aberdeenshire, Scotland, by 1961; sold on behalf of The Haddo House Endowment by The National Trust for Scotland, Christie's, London, July 7, 1978, no. 138; from where purchased by Thomas Agnew and Son, Ltd., London; from where purchased by the Kimbell Art Foundation, Fort Worth, 1980.
6. For a discussion of the attribution and provenance, see Penny 2008, p. 244. For more on the family's collecting, see Smith 2003, pp. 47–52.
7. Martin 1963, pp. 263–66.
8. For the print, see *The Illustrated Bartsch,* vol. 26, p. 13.
9. For a corresponding interpretation, see McTighe 2004, p. 315.
10. See especially Robertson and Whistler 1996, pp. 96–97; and Benati et al. 1999, no. 1.
11. For example, Holland 1961, no. 196. Zapperi 1989, p. 50, does not characterize the Kimbell *Butcher's Shop* as preparatory but does claim that it must have preceded the Oxford version.
12. For this development, see especially McTighe 2004, pp. 310–23.
13. Several of Campi's market scenes are (or were) inscribed with years. According to Lill 1908, p. 137, his *Fish Vendors* at Schloss Fugger, Kirchheim, originally bore the year "1578," which would make it the earliest of his known market scenes with an inscribed year. On the basis of style, Paliaga and De Klerck 1997, p. 174, have argued that Campi's three market scenes in the Pinacoteca di Brera, Milan, were painted before the series that Hans Fugger commissioned from the artist in 1580–81; see note 32 below. For a summation of the arguments, see McTighe 2004, p. 322, n. 1. Regarding Passarotti, his earliest market scenes are usually assigned to about 1580. See note 19 below.
14. Honig 1998, pp. 19–94.
15. Bert W. Meijer, "Cremona e i Paesi Bassi," in Gregori 1985, p. 29.
16. On the provenance of this painting and another market scene by Beuckelaer known to have been in the Farnese collection and gone to Naples, see Fornari Schianchi and Spinosa 1995, pp. 260–62.
17. For an interpretation focusing on the religious significance of Aertsen's *Meat Stall*, see Kavaler 1989, pp. 67–92. See also Wind 1976, p. 93.
18. Gregori 1985, pp. 207–8.
19. The prevailing view is that Passarotti's *Butcher's Shop* dates from about 1580. See Ghirardi 1990, p. 236. For the argument that it dates from around 1577, see Zapperi 1989, p. 66, n. 9. Some have preferred to see it as slightly later, which raises the possibility that it could be a response to the Oxford *Butcher's Shop.* See Robertson 2008, p. 33.
20. On this possibility, see Posner 1971, vol. 1, p. 6. For an alternate view, see Robertson 2008, pp. 31–32.
21. Wind 1974, pp. 25–35. Although dealing with a slightly earlier time, see also Hochmann 1998, pp. 72–76.
22. For this line of interpretation, see Wind 1974, pp. 25–35; Wind 1976, pp. 93–96; and Wind 1977, pp. 108–14.
23. McTighe 2004, pp. 301–23.
24. One of the key figures was Bartolomeo Pisanelli, author of *Trattato della natura de' cibi et del bere*, published in several editions between 1585 and 1619. See McTighe 2004, pp. 307–13.
25. McTighe 2004, p. 311.
26. Ibid., p. 312.

27. Ibid., p. 320.

28. Ibid., pp. 320–21.

29. On Aldrovandi, see Giuseppe Olmi and Paolo Prodi, "Art, Science, and Nature in Bologna Circa 1600," in Bologna, Washington, D.C., and New York 1986, pp. 213–35.

30. For an introduction to *Kunst- und Wunderkammern,* see Impey and MacGregor 1985.

31. On Imperato, see *Dizionario biografico degli Italiani*, vol. 62, pp. 286–90.

32. In 1580, Hans Fugger commissioned a series of market scenes from Campi. See Zamboni 1965, pp. 134–37; and Paliaga and De Klerck 1997, pp. 177–79. For Fugger's interest in the natural sciences and the various *Kunst- und Wunderkammern* that he helped to form, see McTighe 2004, pp. 320–21. Although dealing with Hans's cousin, Hans Jacob Fugger, see also Meadow 2002.

33. McTighe 2004, p. 315.

34. Christiansen 1990, p. 138.

35. For an excellent discussion of the primacy of life study for the young Annibale, see Robertson 1997, pp. 3–42.

36. Zapperi 1989, pp. 52, 54. Passarotti's oeuvre is full of the kind of portraits that might have inspired Annibale. For examples, see Ghirardi 1990, pp. 243–49.

37. Good introductions to life in late Renaissance Bologna include Emiliani 1993, pp. xvii–xxiv; Murphy 2003, pp. 1–12; and Bohn 2004, pp. 9–24.

38. Fanti 1980, pp. 26–27.

39. Ibid., pp. 3–6.

40. The fundamental study of the butchers' guild remains Fanti 1980. On the guild's beginnings, see Fanti 1980, pp. 8–12.

41. Ibid., p. 11. See also Pini 1975, pp. 336–38.

42. Fanti 1980, p. 18. An indication of the importance of the Arte dei Beccai for the protection of Bologna is that, according to records of 1314, the Arte dei Beccai had 990 members in its division of the civil army, while the average for the rest of the eighteen divisions was 320. The second largest division was that of the Società dei Leoni, with 693 members. See Fasoli 1933, p. 46.

43. Fanti 1980, p. 19.

44. Fanti 1974, pp. 224–25.

45. One of these moments came during the political schisms that erupted in Bologna during the late twelfth century between the Geremei (or Guelphs) and Lambertazzi (or Ghibellines). See Fanti 1980, pp. 50–67.

46. Fanti 1980, pp. 56, 66, 68.

47. Ibid., p. 57.

48. For an account of this period in Bologna's history, see Ady 1937.

49. Fanti 1980, p. 117.

50. For an overview of the government, see Mario Fanti, "Bologna nell' età moderna," in Ferri, Benati, Roversi et al. 1978, pp. 216–26.

51. The chapel had been ceded to the butchers' guild in 1463. See Fanti 1980, p. 160; and Pini 1994, p. 97. For the altarpiece, which depicts the Martyrdom of Saint Peter Martyr with the Virgin in Glory and Saints Petronius and Dominic, see Ghirardi 1990, pp. 171–75. For the significance of the subject to the butchers, see Zapperi 1989, p. 47.

52. For a discussion of the Carracci family tree, see Stanzani 1993, pp. 199–203.

53. Fanti 1980, pp. 158, 163, n. 95.

54. On Ludovico's training and early career, see Feigenbaum 1993a, pp. lxxxv–lxxxvii; Bohn 2004, pp. 27–31; and Robertson 2008, pp. 18–21.

55. Malvasia 1841 (ed.), vol. 1, p. 265; Summerscale 2000, p. 86.

56. Zapperi 1989, pp. 45–46.

57. The Carracci are widely thought to have opened their academy in 1582, and Carlo Cesare Malvasia, Annibale's biographer, reports that Ludovico's studio was the first location. See Stanzani 1993, pp. 205–6.

58. Zapperi 1989, pp. 3–5.

59. Ibid., pp. 9–10.

60. Compare the descriptions of the two professions by the sixteenth-century Italian writer Garzoni 1589/1989, pp. 152–53 (butchers), and 817–20 (tailors).

61. Malvasia 1841 (ed.), vol. 1, pp. 265, 271; Summerscale 2000, pp. 86, 102.

62. Zapperi 1989, pp. 3–24. Evidence of Annibale's schooling comes from Malvasia 1841 (ed.), vol. 1, p. 265; Summerscale 2000, p. 86. See also Dempsey 1980, pp. 559–60. The question of Ludovico's education remains unresolved. Owing to his seeming ineloquence as a writer, the general assumption has been that he did not attend grammar school. See Feigenbaum 1993a, p. lxxxv; and Robertson 2008, p. 68.

63. See especially Malvasia 1841 (ed.), vol. 1, p. 327; Summerscale 2000, pp. 250–51. See also Posner 1971, vol. 1, pp. 146–47; and Zapperi 1989, p. 53.

64. More than likely, the *Hunchback Boy* reflects an individual whom Annibale observed on the streets, thought interesting, posed in his studio, and drew. See Robertson and Whistler 1996, p. 107; and Benati et al. 1999, no. 11, who openly wonders if the model is truly hunchbacked. In the context of Annibale's humanity, also of significance are his moving depictions of the blind. See Ottani Cavina 1987, pp. 89–100. Annibale's series of drawings known as *Le Arti di Bologna* (see note 80 below) is often cited as evidence of his sympathies for the less fortunate. For the complexities of viewing the series in this way, see McTighe 1993, pp. 75–91.

65. The story of Annibale being insulted for his relations to butchers appears in Malvasia's *Life* of Pietro Facini; see Malvasia 1841 (ed.), vol. 1, p. 399. The insult was also directed at Annibale's brother, Agostino, who is more likely to have taken offense.

66. Consider the anecdote told by Malvasia in which Annibale openly criticizes Agostino for trying to impress a group of *virtuosi* in Rome, reminding him that he is the son of a tailor. Malvasia 1841 (ed.), vol. 1, pp. 327–28; Summerscale 2000, pp. 250–51.

67. In Florence, the butchers' guild seems to have been equally respected, although it faced mounting obstacles in the form of governmental oversight during the sixteenth century (as was the case also in Bologna). See Andrea Zagli, "Da Beccai a Macellai nella Firenze dei Medici," in Zagli, Mineccia, and Giuntini 2000, pp. 22–28.

68. For example, Wittkower 1952, p. 17, n. 30; and Martin 1963, pp. 264–66. Numerous early accounts of the painting also promote the idea of a group portrait. See Martin 1963, p. 264.

69. For a persuasive rejection, see Posner 1971, vol. 2, p. 4. It is interesting to note that there seems to be at least one sixteenth-century painting of Bolognese origin that can be identified as a group portrait of butchers. See Cavalli-Björkman 1999, pp. 418–19.

70. Of the three Carracci painters, we are best informed about Annibale's youthful appearance. For recent discussions of how the young Annibale looked, see Daniele Benati, "Una vita negli autoritratti," in Benati and Riccòmini 2006, pp. 72–75; and Feigenbaum 2010, pp. 19–38.

71. The year of Vincenzo's birth is unknown. In 1544, he married the seventeen-year-old Francesca Grimaldi. This suggests that he would have been at least in his late fifties by the time of the Oxford *Butcher's Shop*. See Stanzani 1993, p. 199.

72. Fanti 1980, p. 132.

73. For example, Robertson 2008, p. 31.

74. On the Canobbi, see Fanti 1980, pp. 134–36.

75. Fanti 1980, p. 132.

76. This push was instigated by Pier Donato Cesi, vice legate and papal governor of Bologna, who was responsible for major urban reforms during the early 1560s. See Fanti 1980, p. 129. For an overview of the various building projects instigated by Cesi, see Tuttle 1987, pp. 215–46.

77. Fanti 1980, p. 132. For the location of the four "satellite" stalls, see Fanti 1980, p. 161, n. 30.

78. The painting was finished in 1585, and the patron would seem to be Girolamo, who had acquired the chapel in 1584. Annibale's father, Antonio, had lent money to Girolamo's father, Pietro, in 1578. See Zapperi 1989, p. 67, n. 23. According to Fanti 1980, p. 134, the patron of the altarpiece was named Giacomo Canobbi, not Girolamo.

79. Fanti 1980, pp. 136–49; and Zapperi 1989, p. 59.

80. On *Le Arti di Bologna*, see Marabottini 1973, pp. 273–82; Marabottini 1979; and McTighe 1993, pp. 75–91. On the term "straordinario di carne," see Zapperi 1989, p. 68, n. 28. It should be noted that even Vincenzo Carracci was found guilty of short-weighing. See note 87 below.

81. The printmaker was Simon Guillain, and *Le Arti di Bologna* appeared in two editions, one published by Ludovico Grignani, the other by Carl'Antonio Fosarelli.

82. Fanti 1980, p. 146, 150; and Zapperi 1989, p. 59.

83. Fanti 1980, p. 146.

84. Zapperi 1989, p. 60. See also Fanti 1980, p. 155.

85. For the suggestion that the painting represents an attack on Bologna's church leaders for having banned the sale of meat during Lent, see Rossi 1997, pp. 19–35.

86. Miller 1972, pp. 3–7.

87. Zapperi 1989, p. 68, n. 29. Interestingly, the documentation indicates that Vincenzo sold pork, of which there is no sign in the Kimbell *Butcher's Shop*.

88. For an overview of this urban renewal project, see Cristofori and Roversi 1982, pp. 84–85.

89. Cristofori and Roversi 1980, no. 67.

90. The conversion to the fish market seems to have happened by 1772. See an unpublished plan of that year with the vaso grande labeled "pescaria"; Biblioteca comunale dell'Archiginnasio, Bologna, Raccolta Gozzadini, fol. 42, no. 47. According to Cristofori and Roversi 1980, no. 67, a new fish market opened on the same site on May 9, 1815.

91. For the attribution of the map, see De Grazia Bohlin 1979, pp. 118–19. The vaso grande measured 49.40 x 12.60 meters; Fanti 1980, p. 132. For additional information about the dimensions of the site, see Fanti 2000, p. 252.

92. I thank Daniela Schiavina, director of the Biblioteca d'Arte e di Storia di San Giorgio in Poggiale, Bologna, for pointing out to me a fascinating photograph, published in 1929, showing the old vaso grande (then fish market) partially destroyed. At this date, the roof was clearly pitched and supported by wooden beams. The photograph also shows that there were rooms located behind the central hall. See Finelli 1929, p. 152, fig. 192.

93. For the appearance of the guildhall, including a drawn reconstruction, see Rubbiani 1912a, p. 5; and Rubbiani 1912b, p. 5.

94. The vaso piccolo measured 22.80 x 9.12 meters; Fanti 1980, p. 132.

95. The vaso Canobbi measured 41.80 x 12.16 meters; Fanti 1980, p. 132. The original floor plan is partially visible in an eighteenth-century plan recording the southeast corner of the block. There is also a photograph of the north facade from before 1910. See Fanti 1980, pp. 130–31.

96. For an indication of what the typical street-front merchant stall looked like in Renaissance Bologna, see the collection of views from 1601 commissioned by the Ospedale di Santa Maria della Vita, Bologna. For a published illustration of one, see Emiliani 1988, p. 142. I thank Corinna Giudici, director of the Archivio Fotografico della Soprintendenza, Bologna, for bringing the series to my attention.

97. Although the known photographs of the vaso grande and vaso piccolo probably reflect later renovations (see notes 92 and 95 above), it is instructive that both buildings, at least by the late nineteenth century, featured large windows on their facades. The vaso Canobbi had a circular one beneath its pediment; the vaso grande, a semicircular one. It is fully possible that similar windows adorned the original buildings, especially considering that Jacopo da Vignola was involved in Cesi's urban reforms. Vignola practiced an up-to-date style of architecture and would have recognized the suitability of placing large thermal or Serlian windows on the facades of the two complexes. On Vignola in Bologna, see Tuttle 1993, pp. 68–87. Some prints from the early nineteenth century by Antonio Basoli show how well lit Bolognese interiors could be. See Poli and Santucci 2002, pp. 83, 86, and 94. It is also useful to consider the Florentine butchers' hall, located on the Piazza di Mercato Vecchio, with its arcaded clerestory. See Cresti 1998, p. 21.

98. For evidence that, as early as the late thirteenth century, the butchers' guild had sought to centralize slaughter where it was not a bother to the public, see Fanti 1980, pp. 46–47.

99. One indication that slaughter is likely to have been prohibited outside the three butchers' halls near the Porta Ravegnana are the complaints that erupted over attempts in 1669 by Francesco and Giuseppe Azzolini to open a slaughterhouse and butcher's shop in a house to the southwest of the Piazza Maggiore on Via Santa Margherita. After neighbors protested that a slaughterhouse should be allowed to operate so close to their homes, the brothers were forced to relocate their enterprise to a more distant part of the city. See Fanti 1980, pp. 175–76.

100. I am grateful to various butchers in Bologna's Mercato delle Erbe (Via Ugo Bassi, 25) for helping me to identify the carcasses and cuts of meat in the painting.

101. Fanti 1980, pp. 138, 150.

102. See especially Biow 2006, pp. 13–15. Although centered on traditions in France, see also Vigarello 1985, pp. 68–89. Zapperi 1989, pp. 47–48, draws attention to the grayish linens worn by the butchers in Passarotti's *Butcher's Shop* and suggests that the choice of hue was deliberate, a means of emphasizing the lowly and dirty work practiced by the two subjects. For the contrast with Annibale's Oxford *Butcher's Shop*, see Zapperi 1989, p. 58.

103. That hygienic practices were not strictly the purview of the nobility is suggested by the apparent connection between cleanliness in the Netherlands and the rise of commercial dairy farming. See Van Bavel and Gelderblom 2009, pp. 41–69. Another profession that cared about cleanliness and appears to have influenced upper-class habits was the barber-surgeon. See Cavallo 2007.

104. I thank Philip Haas for discussing the making of his film with me. About the project, see Byatt 2009.

105. The fundamental study remains Conisbee 1979, pp. 413–28.

106. For discussions of the development, see Turner 1966; and Gombrich 1966, pp. 107–21.

107. In addition to Leonardo (see note 108 below), Fra Bartolommeo was an important practitioner of plein-air landscape drawing during the Renaissance. See Fischer 1989, pp. 301–42.

108. Turner 1966, pp. 16–18.

109. This concerns a description and annotated diagram by the British painter Richard Symonds of the painting equipment that he found in 1650 in the studio of the Roman painter Giovanni Angelo Canini. See Conisbee 1979, pp. 414–15.

110. There are possible exceptions, and one is the fifteenth-century goldsmith and draftsman Maso Finiguerra, whose graphic oeuvre includes a number of drawings of figures engaged in everyday activities. For the difficulties of determining if any of these drawings were done from life, as well as a survey of other such drawings from the late fifteenth century, see Forlani Tempesti 1994, pp. 1–15.

111. Bambach, Chapman, Clayton, and Goldner 2000, no. 130.

112. There are occasional genre drawings, but none seem plein air. A famous example by Passarotti is his *Two Women Spinning and a Child,* which bears the same comic undertones as his market scenes. See Robertson 2008, pp. 34–35.

113. The canvas is particular in at least one significant regard. It is formed of two pieces that were neatly stitched together. The seam runs vertically and is visible in the X-radiograph near the butcher on the right (fig. 47). For all technical information, see the conservation report prepared in 2001 by Claire Barry, chief conservator at the Kimbell Art Museum, and Isabelle Tokumaru, former associate conservator.

114. Dempsey 2000, pp. 70–73.

115. Malvasia 1841 (ed.), vol. 1, p. 340; Summerscale 2000, p. 277.

116. Malvasia 1841 (ed.), vol. 1, p. 335; Summerscale 2000, p. 269.

117. The main evidence for the trip to Venice is a letter reproduced by Malvasia in which Agostino reports from Venice that Annibale is with him. See Malvasia 1841 (ed.), vol. 1, p. 270; Summerscale 2000, p. 100. The context of the letter points to a date around 1580. For a discussion of the date and why the letter should be accepted as true, see Robertson 2008, pp. 52, 203.

118. For a useful discussion of the *colorito–disegno* debate, see Rosand 1997, pp. 10–25.

119. Ferino-Pagden 2008, pp. 257–58.

120. For an introduction to Titian's painting techniques, see Jill Dunkerton, "Titian's Painting Technique," in Hope 2003, pp. 45–60; and Martina Griesser and Natalia Gustavson, "Observations on Technique and Materials in Titian's Late Work," in Ferino-Pagden 2008, pp. 103–111. On Venetian techniques more generally, see Robert Wald, "Materials and Techniques of Painters in Sixteenth-Century Venice," in Ilchman 2009, pp. 73–81.

121. Recent X-radiography of the Oxford *Butcher's Shop* reveals a similar method of painting. See Robertson 2008, p. 31.

122. The painting was completed by 1548 and placed on view in the Sala Capitolare of the Scuola Grande di San Marco, Venice, which is where Annibale would have seen it. See Pallucchini and Rossi 1982, vol. 1, pp. 34–36, 157–58. For an introduction to Tintoretto's painting techniques, see Jill Dunkerton, "Tintoretto's Painting Technique," in Falomir 2007, pp. 139–58.

123. On the technique of the Oxford *Butcher's Shop,* see Robertson 2008, p. 31. Surprisingly little research has been published on Annibale's painting techniques. For a notable exception, see Ana González Mozo, "Constructing Images of Beauty," in Úbeda de los Cobos, Álvarez-Garcillán Morales, and González Mozo 2005, pp. 73–94, where attention is drawn to the Venetian aspects of the technique. On the Cleveland *Boy Drinking,* see Bologna, Washington, D.C., and New York 1986, pp. 264–65; and Christiansen 1990, pp. 135–45.

124. Bellori 1672, pp. 19–20.

125. The painting was originally located in the church of San Nicolò di San Felice; the year 1583 was only discovered on the bottom edge of the painting in 1923. See Posner 1971, vol. 1, pp. 3–4; vol. 2, pp. 4–5.

126. Malvasia 1841 (ed.), vol. 1, p. 267; Summerscale 2000, pp. 92–93.

127. For the date of the commission, see Boschloo 1974, vol. 2, p. 179. For pertinent stylistic analyses, see Posner 1971, vol. 1, pp. 29–32; and Robertson 2008, p. 46.

128. The degree to which Annibale was deliberately eclectic in his combination of styles has been one of the more hotly contested debates in Carracci scholarship. For a review of the arguments, see Boschloo 1980, pp. 50–54.

129. Benati et al. 1999, no. 8.

130. Robertson 1997, pp. 3–42.

131. See note 57 above.

132. On the Academy, useful discussions include Dempsey 1989, pp. 33–43; Feigenbaum 1990, pp. 145–65; Feigenbaum 1993b, pp. 59–76; and Robertson 2008, pp. 68–77.

133. As made clear by an anonymous drawing in the Nationalmuseum, Stockholm, that doubtlessly represents a drawing session at the Carracci Academy. See Bjurström 2002, pp. 110–11; and Robertson 2008, p. 72.

134. For example, the *Hunchback Boy* at Chatsworth House. See note 64 above. For good discussions of Carracci "academy" drawings, see Feigenbaum 1993b, pp. 64–69; and Robertson 1997, pp. 9–16.

135. Malvasia 1841 (ed.), vol. 1, p. 277; Summerscale 2000, p. 135.

136. He first visited Rome in the fall of 1594 and then returned briefly to Bologna. His permanent move to Rome happened in 1595. On why Annibale was likely chosen, see Robertson 2008, pp. 100–103.

137. On the dating, see Gail Feigenbaum, "Annibale in the Farnese Palace: A Classical Education," in Benati et al. 1999, p. 114. Work on the minor frescoes lasted until 1608.

138. Posner 1971, vol. 1, pp. 100–101, 106.

139. For a discussion of the many influences, not just the Sistine Ceiling, see Posner 1971, vol. 1, pp. 95–102; and Robertson 2008, pp. 165–70.

140. On Annibale's approach to ancient sculpture, see Weston-Lewis 1992, pp. 287–313.

141. Posner 1971, vol. 1, p. 108.

142. Regarding Annibale's preparatory drawings for the Gallery, distinguishing those that reflect life study from those that do not is tricky. For examples of drawings that are sometimes thought to be based on live models, see Benati et al. 1999, nos. 45, 49, 53, 55, 56, and 57. See also Posner 1971, vol. 1, p. 108; and Weston-Lewis 1992, p. 287.

143. Bellori 1672, p. 64, as translated by Posner 1971, vol. 1, p. 108.

Bibliography

Ady 1937
Cecilia M. Ady. *The Bentivoglio of Bologna: A Study in Despotism*. London, 1937.

Bambach, Chapman, Clayton, and Goldner 2000
Carmen C. Bambach, Hugo Chapman, Martin Clayton, and George R. Goldner. *Correggio and Parmigianino: Master Draughtsmen of the Renaissance*. Exh. cat., The British Museum, London; and The Metropolitan Museum of Art, New York. London, 2000.

Bellori 1672
Giovanni Pietro Bellori. *Le vite de' pittori, scultori e architetti moderni: Parte prima*. Rome, 1672.

Benati and Riccòmini 2006
Daniele Benati and Eugenio Riccòmini, eds. *Annibale Carracci*. Exh. cat., Museo Civico Archeologico, Bologna; and the Chiostro del Bramante, Rome. Milan, 2006.

Benati et al. 1999
Daniele Benati, Diane De Grazia, Gail Feigenbaum, Kate Ganz, Margaret Morgan Grasselli, Catherine Loisel Legrand, and Carel van Tuyll van Serooskerken. *The Drawings of Annibale Carracci*. Exh. cat., National Gallery of Art. Washington, D.C., 1999.

Biow 2006
Douglas Biow. *The Culture of Cleanliness in Renaissance Italy*. Ithaca, New York, 2006.

Bjurström 2002
Per Bjurström, ed. *Drawings from the Age of the Carracci: Seventeenth Century Bolognese Drawings from the Nationalmuseum, Stockholm*. Exh. cat., Nationalmuseum, Stockholm; and Ashmolean Museum. Oxford, 2002.

Bohn 2004
Babette Bohn. *Ludovico Carracci and the Art of Drawing*. Turnhout, 2004.

Bologna, Washington, D.C., and New York 1986
The Age of Correggio and the Carracci: Emilian Painting of the Sixteenth and Seventeenth Centuries. Exh. cat., Pinacoteca Nazionale, Bologna; National Gallery of Art, Washington, D.C.; and The Metropolitan Museum of Art, New York. Washington, D.C., 1986. [Italian ed., Bologna, 1986.]

Boschloo 1974
Anton W. A. Boschloo. *Annibale Carracci in Bologna: Visible Reality in Art after the Council of Trent*. 2 vols. The Hague, 1974.

Boschloo 1980
Anton W. A. Boschloo. Review of *Annibale Carracci and the Beginnings of Baroque Style*, by Charles Dempsey. *Simiolus: Netherlands Quarterly for the History of Art* 11, no. 1 (1980), pp. 50–54.

Byam Shaw 1967
James Byam Shaw. *Paintings by Old Masters at Christ Church, Oxford*. London, 1967.

Byatt 2009
A. S. Byatt. *Butchers, Dragons, Gods, and Skeletons: Film Installations by Philip Haas.* Exh. cat., Kimbell Art Museum. Fort Worth, 2009.

Cavalli-Björkman 1999
Görel Cavalli-Björkman. "A Bolognese Portrait of a Butcher." *The Burlington Magazine* 141 (July 1999), pp. 418–19.

Cavallo 2007
Sandra Cavallo. *Artisans of the Body in Early Modern Italy: Identities, Families, and Masculinities.* Manchester, 2007.

Christiansen 1990
Keith Christiansen. "Working from Life in the Accademia dei Desiderosi." In *Scritti in onore di Giuliano Briganti*, pp. 135–45. Milan, 1990.

Conisbee 1979
Philip Conisbee. "Pre-Romantic *Plein-Air* Painting." *Art History* 2, no. 4 (December 1979), pp. 413–28.

Cresti 1998
Matteo Cosimo Cresti. "La tipologia edilizia della bottega fiorentina: Dal Mercato Vecchio al Mercato di San Lorenzo." In Piero Guarducci, Matteo Cosimo Cresti, and Carlo Cresti, *Divagazioni attorno al tema "Carne": Storia, aspetti edilizi, iconografia*, pp. 19–33. Florence, 1998.

Cristofori and Roversi 1980
Franco Cristofori and Giancarlo Roversi, eds. *Le fotografie, 1: Pietro Poppi e la fotografia dell'Emilia.* With contributions by Andrea Emiliani, Giovanni Ricci, and Italo Zannier. Vol. 6, *Le Collezioni d'Arte della Cassa di Risparmio in Bologna.* Bologna, 1980.

Cristofori and Roversi 1982
Franco Cristofori and Giancarlo Roversi, eds. *Le fotografie, 2: Arnaldo Romagnoli: Il volto di Bologna.* With contributions by Carlo di Angelis and Carlo Gentili. Vol. 7, *Le Collezioni d'Arte della Cassa di Risparmio in Bologna.* Bologna, 1982.

De Grazia Bohlin 1979
Diane De Grazia Bohlin. *Prints and Related Drawings by the Carracci Family: A Catalogue Raisonné.* Washington, D.C., 1979.

Dempsey 1980
Charles Dempsey. "Some Observations on the Education of Artists in Florence and Bologna during the Later Sixteenth Century." *The Art Bulletin* 62, no. 4 (December 1980), pp. 552–569.

Dempsey 1989
Charles Dempsey. "The Carracci Academy." In *Academies of Art between Renaissance and Romanticsim*, edited by Anton W. A. Boschloo, Elwin J. Hendrikse, Laetitia C. Smit, and Gert Jan van der Sman, pp. 33–43. *Leids Kunsthistorisch Jaarboek* 5–6, 1986–87. The Hague, 1989.

Dempsey 2000
Charles Dempsey. *Annibale Carracci and the Beginnings of Baroque Style.* 2nd ed. Fiesole, 2000.

Emiliani 1988
Andrea Emiliani, ed. *Dall'avanguardia dei Carracci al secolo barocco: Bologna, 1580–1600.* With contributions by Grazia Agostini et al. Bologna, 1988.

Emiliani 1993
Andrea Emiliani, ed. *Ludovico Carracci.* With contributions by Maria Silva Campanini, Gail Feigenbaum, Sydney J. Freedberg, Giovanna Perini, and Anna Stanzani. Exh. cat., Pinacoteca Nazionale, Bologna; and Kimbell Art Museum, Fort Worth. Bologna, 1993. [English ed., Bologna, 1993.]

Evans and Marr 2006
Robert John Weston Evans and Alexander Marr, eds. *Curiosity and Wonder from the Renaissance to the Enlightenment.* Aldershot, England, and Burlington, Vermont, 2006.

Falomir 2007
Miguel Falomir, ed. *Tintoretto.* Exh. cat., Museo Nacional del Prado. Madrid, 2007.

Fanti 1974
Mario Fanti. *Le Vie di Bologna: Saggio di toponomastica storica e storia della toponomastica urbana.* Bologna, 1974.

Fanti 1980
Mario Fanti. *I Macellai Bolognesi: Mestiere, politica e vita civile nella storia di una categoria attraverso i secoli.* Bologna, 1980.

Fanti 2000
Mario Fanti, ed. *Gli schizzi topografici originali di Giuseppe Guidicini per le Cose Notabili della città di Bologna*. Bologna, 2000.

Fasoli 1933
Gina Fasoli. *Le compagnie delle armi a Bologna*. Bologna, 1933.

Feigenbaum 1990
Gail Feigenbaum. "Drawing and Collaboration in the Carracci Academy." In *IL 60: Essays Honoring Irving Lavin on His Sixtieth Birthday*, edited by Marilyn Aronberg Lavin, pp. 145–65. New York, 1990.

Feigenbaum 1993a
Gail Feigenbaum. "Ludovico Carracci: Un profilo." In Emiliani 1993, pp. lxxxv–cix.

Feigenbaum 1993b
Gail Feigenbaum. "Practice in the Carracci Academy." In *The Artist's Workshop*, edited by Peter M. Lukehart, pp. 59–76. Studies in the History of Art 38. Washington, 1993.

Feigenbaum 2010
Gail Feigenbaum. " 'A likeness in the tomb': Annibale's Self-Portrait Drawing in the J. Paul Getty Museum." *Getty Research Journal* 2 (2010), pp. 19–38.

Ferino-Pagden 2008
Sylvia Ferino-Pagden, ed. *Late Titian and the Sensuality of Painting*. Exh. cat., Kunsthistorisches Museum, Vienna; and Gallerie dell'Accademia. Venice, 2008.

Ferri, Benati, Roversi et al. 1978
Antonio Ferri, Amedeo Benati, Giancarlo Roversi et al. *Storia di Bologna*. Bologna, 1978.

Finelli 1929
Angelo Finelli. *Bologna ai tempi che vi soggiornò Dante, secolo XIII: Aspetto della città con le 180 torri gentilizie allora esistenti; ricostruzione documentata eseguita in rilievo e particolarmente descritta*. Bologna, 1929.

Fischer 1989
Chris Fischer. "Fra Bartolommeo's Landscape Drawings." *Mitteilungen des Kunsthistorischen Institutes in Florenz* 33, no. 2 (1989), pp. 301–42.

Forlani Tempesti 1994
Anna Forlani Tempesti. "Studiare dal naturale nella Firenze di fine '400." In *Florentine Drawing at the Time of Lorenzo the Magnificent: Papers from a Colloquium Held at the Villa Spelman, Florence, 1992*, edited by Elizabeth Cropper, pp. 1–15. Bologna, 1994.

Fornari Schianchi and Spinosa 1995
Lucia Fornari Schianchi and Nicola Spinosa, eds. *I Farnese: arte e collezionismo*. Exh. cat., Palazzo Ducale di Colorno, Parma; Galleria Nazionale di Capodimonte, Naples; and Haus der Kunst, Munich. Milan, 1995.

Furlotti 2000
Barbara Furlotti. *Il carteggio tra Bologna, Parma, Piacenza e Mantova (1563–1634)*. Vol. 4, Le collezioni Gonzaga. Milan, 2000.

Garzoni 1589/1989
Tomaso Garzoni. *La piazza universale di tutte le professioni del mondo*. Ravenna, 1989. [Facsimile edition; originally published, Venice, 1589.]

Ghirardi 1990
Angela Ghirardi. *Bartolomeo Passerotti: Pittore (1529–1592); Catalogo generale*. Rimini, 1990.

Gombrich 1966
E. H. Gombrich. *Norm and Form: Studies in the Art of the Renaissance*. London, 1966.

Gregori 1985
Mina Gregori, ed. *I Campi e la cultura artistica cremonese del Cinquecento*. Exh. cat., Santa Maria della Pietà, Vecchio Ospedale, Cremona; Museo Civico, Sala Manfredini, Cremona. Milan, 1985.

Hochmann 1998
Michel Hochmann. "Genre Scenes by Dosso and Giorgione." In *Dosso's Fate: Painting and Court Culture in Renaissance Italy*, edited by Luisa Ciammitti, Steven F. Ostrow, and Salvatore Settis, pp. 63–82. Los Angeles, 1998.

Holland 1961
Ralph Holland. *The Carracci: Drawings and Paintings*. Exh. cat., The Hatton Gallery, King's College (University of Durham). Newcastle-upon-Tyne, 1961.

Honig 1998
Elizabeth Alice Honig. *Painting and the Market in Early Modern Antwerp.* New Haven, 1998.

Hope 2003
Charles Hope. *Titian.* With contributions from Nicholas Penny, Caroline Campbell, Amanda Bradley et al. Catalogue edited by David Jaffé. Exh. cat., National Gallery. London, 2003.

Ilchman 2009
Frederick Ilchman. *Titian, Tintoretto, Veronese: Rivals in Renaissance Venice.* Exh. cat., Museum of Fine Arts, Boston; and Musée du Louvre, Paris. Boston and New York, 2009.

Impey and MacGregor 1985
Oliver Impey and Arthur MacGregor, eds. *The Origins of Museums: The Cabinet of Curiosities in Sixteenth- and Seventeenth-Century Europe.* Oxford and New York, 1985.

Kavaler 1989
Ethan Matt Kavaler. "Pieter Aertsen's Meat Stall: Divers Aspects of the Market Piece." *Nederlands Kunsthistorisch Jaarboek* 40 (1989), pp. 67–92.

Lapenta and Morselli 2006
Stefania Lapenta and Raffaella Morselli. *Le collezioni Gonzaga: la quadreria nell'elenco dei beni del 1626–1627.* Milan, 2006.

Lill 1908
Georg Lill. *Hans Fugger (1531–1598) und die Kunst.* Leipzig, 1908.

Malvasia 1841 (ed.)
Carlo Cesare Malvasia. *Felsina pittrice: Vite de' pittori Bolognesi.* [1678.] Edited by Giampietro Zanotti. 2 vols. Bologna, 1841.

Marabottini 1973
Alessandro Marabottini. "Sui disegni di Annibale Carracci per le *Arti di Bologna.*" In *Studi offerti a Giovanni Incisa della Rocchetta,* pp. 273–82. Rome, 1973.

Marabottini 1979
Alessandro Marabottini, ed. *Le Arti di Bologna di Annibale Carracci.* Rome, 1979.

Martin 1963
John Rupert Martin. "The Butcher's Shop of the Carracci." *The Art Bulletin* 45, no. 3 (September 1963), pp. 263–66.

McTighe 1993
Sheila McTighe. "Perfect Deformity, Ideal Beauty, and the *Imaginaire* of Work: The Reception of Annibale Carracci's *Arti di Bologna* in 1646." *Oxford Art Journal* 16, no. 1 (1993), pp. 75–91.

McTighe 2004
Sheila McTighe. "Foods and the Body in Italian Genre Paintings, about 1580: Campi, Passarotti, Carracci." *The Art Bulletin* 86, no. 2 (June 2004), pp. 301–23.

Meadow 2002
Mark A. Meadow. "Merchants and Marvels: Hans Jacob Fugger and the Origins of the Wunderkammer." In *Merchants and Marvels: Commerce, Science, and Art in Early Modern Europe,* edited by Pamela H. Smith and Paula Findlen, pp. 182–200. New York, 2002.

Millar 1970–72
Oliver Millar. "The Inventories and Valuations of the King's Goods: 1649–51." *The Walpole Society* 43 (1970–72), pp. 1–458.

Miller 1972
Dwight C. Miller. "'Virtù et Arti Essercitate in Bologna' by Giovanni Maria Tamburini." *Culta Bononia* 4, no. 1 (1972), pp. 3–13.

Murphy 2003
Caroline P. Murphy. *Lavinia Fontana: A Painter and Her Patrons in Sixteenth-Century Bologna.* New Haven, 2003.

Ottani Cavina 1987
Anna Ottani Cavina. "Studies from Life: Annibale Carracci's Paintings of the Blind." In *Emilian Painting of the 16th and 17th Centuries: A Symposium,* edited by Henry A. Millon, pp. 89–103. Bologna, 1987.

Paliaga and De Klerck 1997
Franco Paliaga and Bram De Klerck. *Vincenzo Campi.* Soncino, 1997.

Palluchini and Rossi 1982
Rodolfo Palluchini and Paola Rossi. *Tintoretto: Le opere sacre e profane.* 2 vols. Milan, 1982.

Penny 2008
Nicholas Penny. *The Sixteenth Century Italian Paintings.* Vol. 2, *Venice, 1540–1600.* National Gallery Catalogues. London, 2008.

Perini 1993
Giovanna Perini. "Aggiunte e postille a 'Gli scritti dei Carracci.'" *Accademia Clementina: Atti e memorie* 32 (1993), pp. 127–42.

Pini 1975
Antonio Ivan Pini. "Pesce, pescivendoli e mercanti di pesce in Bologna medievale." *Il Carrobbio* 1 (1975), pp. 329–49.

Pini 1994
Antonio Ivan Pini. "Tra orgoglio civico e 'status symbol': corporazioni d'arte e famiglie aristocratiche in San Petronio nel XIV e XV secolo." In *Una Basilica per una città: Sei secoli in San Petronio,* edited by Mario Fanti and Deanna Lenzi, pp. 87–100. Bologna, 1994.

Poli and Santucci 2002
Marco Poli and Andrea Santucci, eds. *Vedute pittoresche di Bologna di Antonio Basoli: 100 immagini della città ottocentesca.* Bologna, 2002.

Posner 1971
Donald Posner. *Annibale Carracci: A Study in the Reform of Italian Painting around 1590.* 2 vols. National Gallery of Art, Kress Foundation: Studies in the History of European Art. London, 1971.

Robertson 1997
Clare Robertson. "Annibale Carracci and *Invenzione:* Medium and Function in the Early Drawings." *Master Drawings* 35, no. 1 (Spring 1997), pp. 3–42.

Robertson 2008
Clare Robertson. *The Invention of Annibale Carracci.* Milan, 2008.

Robertson and Whistler 1996
Clare Robertson and Catherine Whistler. *Drawings by the Carracci from British Collections.* Exh. cat., The Ashmolean Museum, Oxford; and Hazlitt, Gooden & Fox. London, 1996.

Rosand 1997
David Rosand. *Painting in Sixteenth-Century Venice: Titian, Veronese, Tintoretto.* Rev. ed. Cambridge and New York, 1997.

Rossi 1997
Francesca Rossi. "La 'Macelleria' di Annibale Carracci e il bando per la quaresima del cardinale Gabriele Paleotti." *Paragone* 48 (1997), pp. 19–35.

Rubbiani 1912a
Alfonso Rubbiani. "Del restauro del Palazzo dell'Arte dei Beccai." [Pt. 1.] *Il Resto del Carlino,* March 27, 1912, p. 5.

Rubbiani 1912b
Alfonso Rubbiani. "Del restauro del Palazzo dell'Arte dei Beccai." [Pt. 2.] *Il Resto del Carlino,* March 28, 1912, p. 5.

Smith 2003
Claire Smith. "The 4th Earl of Aberdeen as a Collector of Italian Old Masters." *Journal of the Scottish Society for Art History* 8 (2003), pp. 47–52.

Stanzani 1993
Anna Stanzani. "Regesto della vita e delle opere." In Emiliani 1993, pp. 199–268.

Summerscale 2000
Anne Summerscale. *Malvasia's Life of the Carracci: Commentary and Translation.* University Park, Pennsylvania, 2000.

Turner 1966
A. Richard Turner. *The Vision of Landscape in Renaissance Italy.* Princeton, 1966.

Tuttle 1987
Richard J. Tuttle. "*Bononia Resurgens*: A Medallic History by Pier Donato Cesi." In *Italian Medals,* edited by J. Graham Pollard, pp. 215–46. Studies in the History of Art 21. Washington, D.C., 1987.

Tuttle 1993
Richard J. Tuttle. "Vignola's Facciata dei Banchi in Bologna." *Journal of the Society of Architectural Historians* 52, no. 1 (March 1993), pp. 68–87.

Úbeda de los Cobos, Álvarez-Garcillán Morales, and González Mozo 2005
Andrés Úbeda de los Cobos, María Álvarez-Garcillán Morales, and Ana González Mozo. *Annibale Carracci's Venus, Adonis and Cupid*. Exh. cat., Museo Nacional del Prado. Madrid, 2005.

Van Bavel and Gelderblom 2009
Bas van Bavel and Oscar Gelderblom. "The Economic Origins of Cleanliness in the Dutch Golden Age." *Past and Present* 205 (November 2009), pp. 41–69.

Vigarello 1985
Georges Vigarello. *Le propre et le sale: L'hygiène du corps depuis le Moyen Age*. Paris, 1985.

Weston-Lewis 1992
Aidan Weston-Lewis. "Annibale Carracci and the Antique." *Master Drawings* 30 (1992), pp. 287–313.

Wind 1974
Barry Wind. "*Pitture ridicole*: Some Late Cinquecento Comic Genre Paintings." *Storia dell'Arte* 20 (1974), pp. 25–35.

Wind 1976
Barry Wind. "Annibale Carracci's 'Scherzo': The Christ Church *Butcher Shop*." *The Art Bulletin* 58, no. 1 (March 1976), pp. 93–96.

Wind 1977
Barry Wind. "Vincenzo Campi and Hans Fugger: A Peep at Late Cinquecento Bawdy Humor." *Arte Lombarda* 47–48 (1977), pp. 108–14.

Wittkower 1952
Rudolf Wittkower. *The Drawings of the Carracci in the Collection of Her Majesty the Queen at Windsor Castle*. London, 1952.

Zagli, Mineccia, and Giuntini 2000
Andrea Zagli, Francesco Mineccia, and Andrea Giuntini. *"Maledetti beccari": Storia dei macellai fiorentini dal Cinquecento al Duemila*. Florence, 2000.

Zamboni 1965
Silla Zamboni. "Vincenzo Campi." *Arte Antica e Moderna* 30 (1965), pp. 124–47.

Zapperi 1989
Roberto Zapperi. *Annibale Carracci: Ritratto di artista da giovane*. Turin, 1989.